Views In and Around Kyoto (Rakuchū rakugai-zu)—Ikeda version (detail). Hayashibara Museum of Art. Photo: Hayashibara Museum of Art / DNPartcom

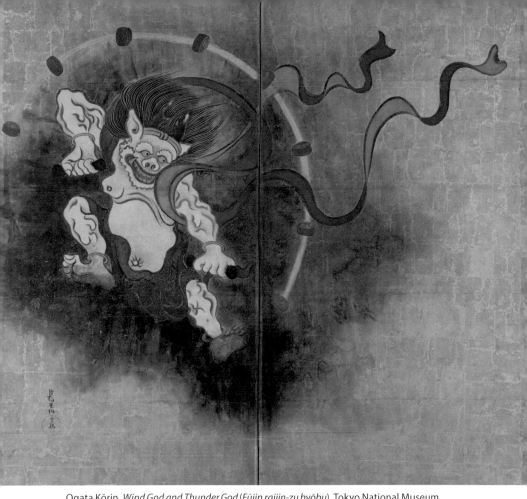

Ogata Kōrin, *Wind God and Thunder God* (*Fūjin raijin-zu byōbu*). Tokyo National Museum. Image: TNM Image Archives

Kanō Osanobu. *Agriculture in the Four Seasons* (*Shiki kōsaku-zu byōbu*). Suntory Museum of Art.

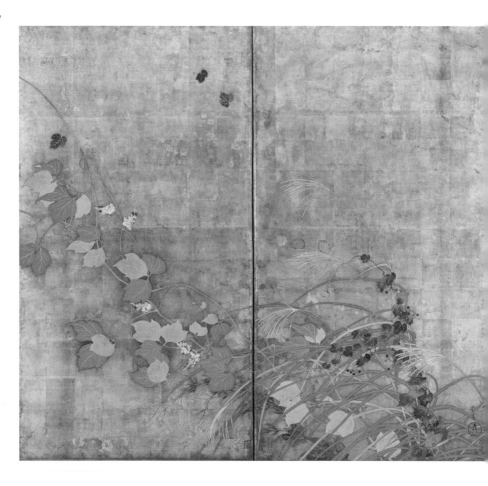

Sakai Hōitsu, *Flowering Plants of Summer and Autumn* (*Natsu-aki kusa-zu byōbu*). Tokyo National Museum. Image: TNM Image Archives

Ogata Kōrin, *Red and White Plum Blossoms* (*Kōhakubai-zu byōbu*). MOA Museum of Art.

Kanō Tan'yū, *Pines of the Four Seasons* (*Shiki matsu-zu byōbu*).
Daitokuji temple. Image: Kyoto National Museum

Ogata Kōrin, *Irises* (*Kakitsubata-zu byōbu*) (right screen). Nezu Museum.

Anonymous, *Birds and Flowers in Autumn and Winter* (*Shūtō kachō-zu byōbu*). Suntory Museum of Art.

Sesshū, *Landscapes of the Four Seasons* (*Shiki sansui-zu maki*) (detail). Mohri Museum.

Yasui Sōtarō, *Portrait of Chin-Jung (Kin'yō)*. National Museum of Modern Art, Tokyo. Photo: MOMAT / DNPartcom

Takahashi Yuichi, *Reader and Notebook (Tokuhon to sōshi)*. Kotohiragū Shrine Museum.

Jean-Auguste-Dominique Ingres, *Portrait of Philibert Rivière (Monsieur Philibert Rivière)*. Musée du Louvre, Paris. Photo © RMN-Grand Palais (Musée du Louvre) / Franck Raux / Distributed by AMF-DNPartcom

Takahashi Yuichi, *Salmon (Sake)*. The University Art Museum, Tokyo University of the Arts. Photo: The University Art Museum, Tokyo University of the Arts / DNPartcom

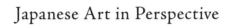

Japanese Art in Perspective

JAPAN LIBRARY

Japanese Art *in* Perspective

East-West Encounters

TAKASHINA Shūji

Translated by Matt Treyvaud

Japan Publishing Industry Foundation for Culture

Note to the reader: For Japanese words, long vowels are indicated by macrons, except in familiar place names. The custom of placing the family name first has been followed for Japanese names.

Japanese Historical Periods

ca. 14,000–1,000 BCE	Jōmon		1336–1573	Muromachi
ca. 1,000 BCE–300 CE	Yayoi		1573–1603	Azuchi-Momoyama
300–538	Kofun		1603–1868	Edo
538–710	Asuka		1868–1912	Meiji
710–794	Nara		1912–1926	Taishō
794–1185	Heian		1926–1989	Shōwa
1185–1333	Kamakura		1989–2019	Heisei
1333–1336	Kenmu Restoration		2019–present	Reiwa

Japanese Art in Perspective: East-West Encounters
Takashina Shūji. Translated by Matt Treyvaud.

Published by
Japan Publishing Industry Foundation for Culture (JPIC)
2-2-30 Kanda-Jinbocho, Chiyoda-ku, Tokyo 101-0051, Japan

First English edition: March 2021

This book is a translation of *Zōho Nihon bijutsu o miru me: Higashi to nishi no deai,* which was published by Iwanami Shoten, Publishers, Tokyo, first in hardcover in 1991, followed by a paperback edition in 1996, and then republished in 2009 with additional essays.
English publishing rights arranged with Iwanami Shoten, Publishers, Tokyo.

Jacket and cover design: Okamoto Yōhei
Jacket and cover illustration: Ogata Kōrin. *Wind God and Thunder God* (detail), eighteenth century. Tokyo National Museum. Image: TNM Image Archives.
Sakai Hōitsu. *Flowering Plants of Summer and Autumn* (detail), nineteenth century. Tokyo National Museum. Image: TNM Image Archives.

Printed in Japan
ISBN 978-4-86658-180-4
https://japanlibrary.jpic.or.jp/

Preface to the English Edition

At the beginning of *The Waste Land*, T.S. Eliot describes new life rising from the land in spring with the phrase "mixing / Memory and desire." The Japanese, too, have cultivated a unique sense of beauty that mixes memories of the past with the desire for a new future, on the one hand expressing in a variety of life-affirming arts their joy in the natural cycle of the seasons, while on the other seeking new possibilities in external cultures—in ancient times, China, and since the modern period, the advanced countries of the West.

Consider the epochal Japanese invention of kana characters and culture. After adopting kanji, the writing system of the advanced ancient civilization of China, the Japanese found a new use for the characters, using them to represent sound rather than meaning even as they continued diligently studying Chinese poetry and prose. Eventually this usage passed through the intermediate stage of *man'yōgana* to arrive at what we today call kana. This allowed the Japanese to record and pass on the fruits of their efforts at "mixing memory and desire" in their native language. The written word preserved narratives like the *Tale of Genji* and *Tales of Ise*, collections of essays like the *Pillow Book* and *Essays in Idleness*, records of daily life like diaries and travelogues, and above all the vast poetic riches of the *Kokinshū* (Collection of old and new Japanese poems) and other imperial anthologies of poetry over the generations—not to mention later forms of poetry that arose from this heritage, including haiku. The particular sensitivity and aesthetic consciousness that gave rise to this literary world also supported many other endeavors: paintings on picture-scrolls and folding screens, musical works in genres ranging from *yōkyoku* to *sōkyoku*, theatrical traditions like noh and kabuki, shrine and temple architecture, crafts like earthenware and lacquerware, cultural practices like the tea ceremony and ikebana, annual observances like festivals and seasonal celebrations, and everyday rituals and etiquette—in short, every aspect of Japanese culture.

For many years now, I have sought to unravel and explain Japanese aesthetics from a range of perspectives in my varied roles as an organizer of exhibitions of Japanese art in France and elsewhere, a participant in international symposia and academic lectures, and simply as an individual conversing with friends from the West. This book gathers the articles, speeches, and essays prepared on those occasions into a single volume. It is my sincere desire that these writings help broaden understanding of the Japanese sense of beauty that gave rise to, and still underlies, the arts of Japan.

Takashina Shūji

CONTENTS

8

Part III
PASSING BEAUTY, RETURNING MEMORY 137

Part I

METHODS OF JAPANESE ART

1. The Character of Japanese Aesthetics

— 1 —

The Japanese word *utsukushii* is most commonly translated into English as "beautiful," but it did not always have its present meaning. According to linguist Ōno Susumu's *Nihongo no nenrin* (The growth rings of Japanese, Yūki Shobō, 1961), in ancient Japan the word expressed feelings of affection toward parents or family members. This can be seen in examples such as this passage from a poem by Yamanoue no Okura in the eighth-century *Man'yōshū* anthology:

> *meko mireba*   . . . when one sees one's wife and children,
> *megushi utsukushi*   they inspire tenderness, affection . . .

During the Heian period, the meaning of the word shifted to express feelings of affection for small and delicate things, perhaps similar to the English word "adorable." When the supernatural Princess Kaguya is discovered in a bamboo stalk in the tenth-century *Tale of the Bamboo Cutter*, she is described as "just three inches (*sun*) tall, and *utsukushii*"; the renowned *Pillow Book* of Sei Shōnagon declares that "anything and everything small is *utsukushi*." It was not until the Muromachi period that the term began to be used with something close to its present meaning.

What, then, was the ancient word for "beauty"? Ōno reports that it was *kuwashi* in the Nara period and *kiyora* in the Heian period. The latter evolved from the word *kiyoshi*, a word meaning "pure" in the sense of "unsullied" or "unclouded" that is still used in its modern form, *kiyoi*. *Kuwashi* survives in slightly modified form as an element in the modern word *kaguwashii*, "fragrant," but its direct descendent is *kuwashii*: "detailed," or "fine." The now-common Sino-Japanese word *kirei* first appeared in the Muromachi period, also with the original meaning "unsullied" or simply "clean."

Ōno concludes his analysis as follows:

> Throughout this transition from *kuwashi* to *kiyora* to *utsukushi* to *kirei*, it seems that Japanese ideas of beauty were attuned less to what is good or abundant than what is pure, clean, or fine.

This idiosyncrasy that Ōno identified in the history of the Japanese language itself, intriguingly enough, speaks to the unique character of the Japanese sense of beauty that survives to this day. That character is, first, highly emotional and sentimental, as is evident from the origin of *utsukushi* in feelings of affection. Second, as words like *kuwashi* and *kiyoshi* indicate, the Japanese find much more beauty in what is small, lovely, or immaculate than what is big, strong, or abundant. By contrast, the ancient Greek ideals from which the Western sense of beauty arose did link beauty to strength and abundance.

Indeed, to the ancient Greeks, beauty was an ideal. Like goodness and truth, it belonged to the gods, who were above humanity. This made it easy to draw connections between beauty and other ideals such as strength and wisdom. In Greek mythology, the Judgment of Paris is essentially a beauty contest in which two of the competing goddesses, Hera and Athena, promise Paris wealth, power, and wisdom if he will declare them the most beautiful of all. Similarly, most of the men depicted in Greek art and sculpture are either gods, heroes, or victors at the Olympic Games, indicating a natural overlap between admiration for beauty and admiration for strength. Put bluntly, the beauty of Greek sculpture is undergirded by the glorification of strength.

Such ideas were not limited to ancient Greece. In China, too, the character for "beauty" (美) originally represented a large (大) sheep (羊). Another character meaning "beautiful" or "glorious" (麗) represented a deer (鹿) with exceptionally large antlers. Beauty was linked to size. This sense that large and strong things were beautiful, however, appears to have been lacking in Japan. In a critical essay entitled "Kiyōmono no sekai" ("The world of the virtuosi," collected in *Nihon bunka kenkyū* [Studies in Japanese culture], Shinchōsha, 1959), Kawakita Michiaki describes visiting an exhibition of ancient Japanese art in Rome and finding that even the art of the Momoyama period, known in Japan for its splendor and magnificence, seemed delicate and dainty against the backdrop of the city. Kawakita was surprised by this, but his impressions were surely accurate. Compared to the countless works of art born of the Western sense of beauty, the art of Japan, even the sumptuous screen and sliding-door paintings of the Momoyama period, is on the whole rather gentle and charming.

What is more, in the West—at least until the appearance of the Romantic aesthetic in the late eighteenth century—beauty was linked to rationality and pursued in mathematics, geometry, mechanics, and other fields. The ancient Greeks sought a basis for the beauty of the human form in mathematical proportions, and the Renaissance saw repeated attempts to reduce beauty to geometric principles. The nineteenth-century Neoclassical painter Jacques-Louis David claimed that beauty could only be expressed with the "lamp of reason" as a guide. His friend the theorist Quatremère de Quincy invoked the same rationalist tradition when he argued for "treating the arts the same way as the sciences."

In short, Western classicism (again, until the Romantic era) sought to understand beauty in terms of objective, rational principles. In this context, the emotional, sentimental ideas of beauty held by the Japanese appear even more remarkable. Symmetry, proportion, geometry, the Golden Ratio—the history of Japanese aesthetics includes no attempts to reduce the idea of beauty to such rational principles. This is because beauty was understood not as an inherent quality but rather as something that existed solely within the heart of the person who felt it. The preface of the tenth-century *Kokinshū* anthology, which begins, "Japanese poetry has the human heart as its seed and grows into myriad leaves of words," is arguably the first manifesto for this aesthetic, but it was far from the last. From poet and editor Fujiwara no Teika, whose 1219 treatise *Maigetsushō* (Monthly notes) identifies verse "with feeling" (*ushintai*) as the poetic ideal and instructs the reader to "choose words with feeling as foundation," through noh actor, playwright, and theorist Zeami, whose fifteenth-century *Teachings on Style and the Flower* (*Fūshikaden*) observes that "what is felt to be unusual is what fascinates," to Motoori Norinaga's eighteenth-century theory of *mono no aware*, sometimes translated as "the pathos of things," an "aesthetic of sentiment" has always played an important part in the history of Japanese aesthetics.

One consequence of this view, which posits beauty not as an inherent characteristic of the subject but instead as a part of the world of feeling the subject evokes, is that the nature of the subject is not of great concern. Just as parental love for a child is not inspired by the perfection of that child's features, Japanese aesthetic feeling does not demand the Golden Ratio or bodies that are exactly eight heads high. On the contrary, the heart that knows beauty may find it in the mountains and rivers, the grasses and trees, or any of the myriad things in the world. The *Kokinshū* preface describes poetry as "the expression of how people feel in their hearts about what they see and hear," but what is seen or heard need not be perfect or flawless for this expression to be beautiful. From this we arrive at ideas like those found in the *Essays in Idleness*: "Must we view flowers only when in high bloom, the moon only when full?" and "Once the silk trimming has come loose and the mother-of-pearl fallen from its spindle, then [the scroll] is truly special." This is the birth of awareness of the beauty of the imperfect, the incomplete, even the abandoned. The Western classical aesthetic gave rise to "idealized landscapes" by seventeenth-century painters like Claude Lorrain and Nicolas Poussin, who saw nature as it actually exists as incomplete, and therefore amended and augmented it to grant it the form it "should" have. In Japan, on the other hand, every one of nature's ever-changing aspects was viewed as deeply fascinating, and the tendency to find some unique beauty in each was strong. This, too, surely bears some connection to the aforementioned "aesthetic of sentiment."

— 2 —

The Japanese sense of beauty is, naturally, reflected in the world of Japanese art. We might point to a strong predilection for small, delicate, and miniaturized forms as a major characteristic of expressions of beauty in Japan. Indeed, miniaturization appeals strongly to Japanese tastes in many domains. Gardens are landscaped to evoke "deep mountains and dark valleys" (as the standard phrasing goes) in just a few square meters, and hobbies such as bonsai and *hakoniwa* (literally, "box-gardens"), once unique to Japan, are now known around the world. In the field of crafts in particular, techniques were developed to permit meticulously refined expressiveness in the finest details of *maki-e* lacquerware, dyed textiles, pottery, metalwork, and woodwork. The Japanese of centuries ago who adored these exquisite, delicate pieces surely admired the sheer brilliance of the workmanship required, but they must also have found much beauty in them.

This idea of beauty is also clearly visible in the world of painting. Painting in Japan has always had a tendency to incorporate craft-inspired elements, from the liberal use of gold foil in ancient Buddhist painting to the gold, silver, and pure white fields in folding screen paintings of the early modern era. However, looking beyond the technical aspects of creating the physical artwork, an affection for miniaturization is often evident in spatial composition and how the subject is depicted. Early modern screen paintings that teem with countless tiny figures in everyday situations are an excellent example.

Compared to Western art, Japanese painting is often described as flat, decorative, and lacking in realism. It is true that such paintings are not "realistic" in the sense that they know nothing of the unified, three-dimensional spaces made possible by the development of perspective and shading techniques that began in the West during the Renaissance. This is precisely why, starting in the second half of the eighteenth century, Japanese artists like Shiba Kōkan were so stunned when they encountered Western images that sought to realistically represent the world in this way. However, earlier

Views In and Around Kyoto (Rakuchū rakugai-zu)—Ikeda version (detail). Hayashibara Museum of Art. Photo: Hayashibara Museum of Art / DNPartcom

Japanese artists did not lack the urge toward "realism" in the sense of observing the real world and striving to re-create it. The realism of Japanese artists is found in details rather than overall spatial composition, a fact not unconnected to the aesthetic delight that the Japanese take in miniaturized worlds.

Consider the compositions used in folding screen paintings that depict scenes from everyday life. Popular in the early modern period, these paintings include the "in and around the capital" (*rakuchū rakugai*) genre in general as well as depictions of specific locations like Shijō Kawaramachi in Kyoto or events such as festivals. In these paintings, the emphasis is not on the overall composition but rather on the minute depiction of countless details. Most take urban life, particularly life in Kyoto, as their subject, and therefore contain temples, merchants, streetscapes, and bridges, all viewed as if from high above the clouds. However, this is not the "bird's-eye view" of Western art, in which techniques of perspective are used to render a whole town as if seen from a single point. In these folding screen paintings, every building and street is viewed from roughly the same angle, regardless of where in the image it is located. In other words, the painter is not "viewing" the scene from a fixed point in the sky, but rather roaming freely above the streets of the whole town. Moreover, while the buildings are drawn from relatively high angles, as if to set the overall stage, the scenes that play out on that stage are not. On the contrary: the monkey-handlers, street performers, and passersby are all carefully drawn as if the artist were standing right beside them. Tiny as they are, they are so detailed that you can even make out the patterns on their kimonos. A scene truly viewed from far above could not be depicted in such detail or from such close range. The people in these paintings are not small because they are distant. They are small because they have been miniaturized.

These precisely miniaturized worlds unfolding across every part of the image prevent the emergence of a unified scene in the Western sense. A classically integrated composition of the sort mastered in the Renaissance is an image of the world seen from a single point of view. Theories of perspective are generally based on principles of correspondence between distance within the imagined space, size on the canvas, and darkness of color. Distant things appear small to us, and near things large; therefore, the size of an object in a painting is determined by its distance from the painter. Similarly, because near things appear brightly colored while distant ones appear faint and vague, the richness of color used to depict an object also depends on distance. Tiny human figures in a painting are not miniature people; they are simply far away. Their clothing is painted in muted hues not because it is dirty but, again, because it is distant. The depiction of each figure and object in the painting is appropriate to its proximity, and a unified space with three-dimensional depth emerges as a result.

This kind of unified composition is premised on a single, unmoving painterly perspective. This requirement is absolute and unavoidable. "Near" and "far" are conceived relative to the painter, so any movement on the painter's part will alter the spatial relationships structuring the painting. However, a Japanese "in and around the capital" painting is a sort of anthology of details, devoid of any fixed perspective. The city as a whole is viewed from above, but the figures within it seem to be right before us. The painter's theoretical standpoint when drawing a monkey-handler on the right is unconnected to the standpoint adopted when drawing a festival procession on the left. The painter's "eye" roams freely through the imagined Kyoto streets, allowing the painter to draw everything they see from near enough to distinguish patterns on clothing. We might even say that it moves through the city *in order to* view each scene at close range. The result is far from a unified space, but every part of the painting is filled with realistic detail.

— 3 —

Along with dainty miniaturization, appeals to the Japanese tendency to see beauty in the pure and immaculate are also widespread in the nation's art. The plain wooden architecture of Ise Grand Shrine is one example. Another example from visual art is the emphasis on margins and white spaces that contain nothing at all. As noted earlier, the word *kiyora* originally referred to an unsullied, unclouded state. In other words, it described not the *presence* of goodness or abundance, but the *absence* of unnecessary or unpleasant elements. We might call this an "aesthetic of negation." The present tendency to find rich, deep beauty in ink wash paintings, which reject a diversity of color in favor of monotone shades of ink, or on the noh stage, where extravagant props and movements are reduced to the bare minimum, is an inheritance from the ancient Japanese who found pure things beautiful. When tea master Sen no Rikyū heard that Hideyoshi, by then the ruler of all Japan, wished to see the morning glories in his garden, and then destroyed them all save for a single bloom which he displayed in the tokonoma alcove when he received Hideyoshi, this, too, was rooted in the aesthetic of negation. It should go without saying that this aesthetic shares much with the aesthetic notions of *wabi* and *sabi*, which emphasize humbleness and restraint.

The combination of this aesthetic of negation, which cuts away all unnecessary elements, with the previously discussed fondness for small things, spurred the development of a unique technique in which a single natural

Jan Brueghel the Elder, *Still Life with Flowers* (*Stilleven met bloemen*). Kunsthistorisches Museum. Photo © Kunsthistorisches Museum Wien c/o DNPartcom

subject is isolated for depiction in close detail. Traditional Japanese art includes countless images of flowers and other plants treated in precisely this way. Western art often takes flora as its subject, too, but it tends to be depicted in connection with its surroundings: consider the field of spring flowers in Botticelli's *Primavera*, or the vases and tables in seventeenth-century Dutch still lifes or works by Jan Brueghel the Elder. In Japan, however, pictures of flowers or plants are just that: pictures depicting *only* flowers or plants—and often only a small part of the plant, at that—with the entire surrounding context cut away. For example, in Sakai Hōitsu's *Flowering Plants of Summer and Autumn* (*Natsu-aki kusa-zu byōbu*)—one of the best-known examples of this genre, painted around 1820—the foreground flora is drawn with meticulous care, but, aside from a stylized water current, nothing else is depicted at all. There is no earth, no fields, no sky; the only element other than the main motif is an abstract silver field. It is evident from how the flowering plants are painted that they are outside, but the image contains no

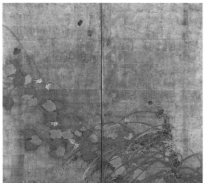

Sakai Hōitsu, *Flowering Plants of Summer and Autumn* (*Natsu-aki kusa-zu byōbu*).
Tokyo National Museum. Photo: TNM Image Archives

landscape features to show this.

Gold and silver backgrounds were also used in genre paintings and portraits. Highly prized by patrons, they are also a fine symbol of the distinctive character of Japanese art. On one hand, they have a brilliant, ornamental effect; on the other, they serve to abbreviate and simplify—to eliminate everything but the main subject. The *tagasode* (literally "whose sleeves?") genre, in which kimono hanging on racks are depicted with a marvelous combination of detail and ornament, obviously featured indoor scenes. The Matsuura folding screen paintings also depict indoor scenes, while the Hikone screen depicts motifs that are partly inside and partly outside. None of these works, however, contain any additional context to indicate whether they take place indoors or outdoors.

By contrast, Western genre paintings, such as those from seventeenth-century Holland, include many such hints: If the scene is inside, the painting will show the interior of the building in the form of its walls, floor, or ceiling. Outdoor scenes have streetscapes or scenery in the background. In either case, the real world surrounding the main subject is represented using a variety of elements. In Japanese genre paintings, however, artists came to focus solely on the main motifs, covering everything else with a field of silver or gold.

Western Kings on Horseback (Taisei ōkō kiba zu) (detail). Kobe City Museum. Photo: Kobe City Museum / DNPartcom

"Emperor Otho," from *Roman Emperors on Horseback* (based on prints by Stradanus). The Elisha Whittelsey Collection, The Elisha Whittelsey Fund, 1949.

The seventeenth-century *Western Kings on Horseback* (*Taisei ōkō kiba zu*) paintings on folding screens held by the Suntory Museum of Art and Kobe City Museum provide an intriguing example of this difference. The mounted figures that are the central subjects of these works are clearly based on Western models. Researchers have even identified a direct source for some of them, to wit: Western prints based on Stradanus's *Roman Emperors on Horseback* series. However, while the original prints include scenes from Rome as the backdrop to their mounted emperors, the Japanese artist of the *Western Kings* series copied only the mounted figures. The original background is replaced with a bare, monochrome plain beneath a sky-like gold field. In other words, nearly everything except the main subject is cut cleanly away.

This intense focus on isolated motifs eventually gave rise to another unique compositional technique in Japanese art: framing only a very small

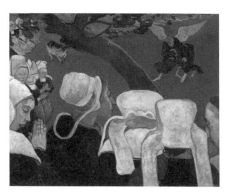

Paul Gauguin, *Vision After the Sermon* (*Vision après le sermon*). Scottish National Gallery, Edinburgh. Photo: Bridgeman Images / DNPartcom

Utagawa Hiroshige, "Plum Estate, Kameido" (*Kameido umeyashiki*). Photo: ColBase (https://colbase.nich.go.jp/)

part *of* the motif. Japanese "paintings of flowers and birds" (*kachō ga*) derive from a Chinese genre known as "broken-off branch paintings" (*zhézhī huā*), which depict only a single branch of a tree, leaving out the trunk and other branches. Starting around the Momoyama period, Japanese folding and sliding screen paintings often featured compositions in which tree trunks, if shown at all, were cut off by the edge of the image. In Hiroshige's ukiyo-e print "Plum Estate, Kameido" (*Kameido umeyashiki*), the foreground is dominated by a small section of a large plum tree's trunk. We know how fresh and unusual Western painters found bold compositions like this from the extent to which they drew direct inspiration from them. Van Gogh made a copy of Hiroshige's print in oils, and the print also influenced his painting *The Sower* as well as Gauguin's *Vision After the Sermon*. It is well known that many Western painters in the latter half of the nineteenth century admired and were influenced by ukiyo-e, and particularly by their composition. Images framed to show just part of the subject were viewed as highly, and distinctively, Japanese.

— 4 —

In paintings such as those in the "in and around the capital" genre, where the artist's perspective moves freely so that all detail is viewed from the same angle and there is no unified spatial composition, the image tends to expand flatly outward to the left and right as far as it can. This contrasts with the Western approach in which, as clearly stated in Leon Battista Alberti's fifteenth-century *On Painting* (*De pictura*), the painter views the world framed in an orderly fashion from a single, fixed perspective, as if looking through a window. In fact, that "window" is nothing less than the painting itself. Just like the painter's fixed perspective, the edges of the painting are a necessary prerequisite for a unified composition.

In Japanese pictorial composition, however, the artist's perspective moves freely, and in principle the image can follow this movement and expand without limit. In reality, of course, the physical edges of the medium—a folding screen or sliding room partition, say—preclude this, but in conceptual terms, the world represented within those borders tends to expand beyond them, outside what is visible within the physical "frame." In works that focus on a close-up of the subject, too—like the "broken-off branch paintings" described above—the parts not painted are still imagined. This allows the work to evoke a world extending beyond its physical bounds.

Put another way, the edges of a classical Western painting are fundamental bounds within which a complete world exists—a microcosm entirely cut off from the outside. But the edges of a Japanese painting are less restrictive borders because, even if the medium itself imposes physical limitations, the framing of the work always suggests something beyond it.

The best example of this is the *emakimono* or "picture-scroll." Much beloved in Japan, picture-scrolls were designed to be viewed by slowly unrolling one edge while rolling up the other. The image depicted thus unfolds in a continuous stream that progresses slowly before the eyes of the viewer. At no point is any "frame" clearly indicated. It is easy to see how a format like this would, as part of its fundamental character, assume a mobile perspective. In

Legends of Mount Shigi (*Shigisan engi*) picture-scroll. Chōgosonshiji temple. Image: National Diet Library Collections

a picture-scroll, the artist's perspective moves constantly and continuously. By unrolling the scroll to make the image move, the viewer follows along.

It is common for a picture-scroll to depict the travels of its protagonist, showing the landscape change as he or she moves from place to place, as in well-known scrolls such as the *Shigisan Engi* (Legends of Mount Shigi) and *Ippen Hijiri-e* (Illustrated life of the priest Ippen). The physical characteristics of the picture-scroll suit it well to this task. As the protagonist travels from mountain to village, or from one town to the next, the physical journey and the passage of time it implies are depicted as part of a continuity of spatial expression. Picture-scrolls visually represent stories and may include a variety of locations as the story unfolds, but no clear boundary line separates one image from the next.

Scroll-format paintings were not unknown in the West, but the format fell out of use at an extremely early stage. Works expressing a story that unfolded over a period of time might arrange scenes alongside each other, but as strictly separate images instead of a single continuum. For example, when Michelangelo painted the story of creation on the ceiling of the Sistine

Chapel, he began by dividing the ceiling into segments with architectural motifs, then drew an independent image in each segment. The images are distinct from each other and entirely lack the natural continuity of a Japanese picture-scroll. This illustrates the difference between the Japanese and Western conceptions of space, and the differences in aesthetic sensibilities that arise as a result.

The picture-scroll format was ideal for representing continuous spaces such as the scenery on a journey. Put the other way around, we might say that the popularity of the picture-scroll in Japan reflects how strongly the Japanese conceive of space as a continuity. Indeed, the picture-scroll format was beloved not just in the Heian and Kamakura periods but for centuries afterward, well into the modern period. For example, the genre includes masterpieces like Shimomura Kanzan's 1908 *Imperial Visit to Ōhara* (*Ōhara gokō*) and Yokoyama Taikan's 1923 *Metempsychosis* (*Seisei ruten*). This same awareness of spatial continuity is also apparent in other areas of Japanese art and culture.

For example, Japanese architecture does not delineate "inside" and "outside" as strictly as its Western counterpart. A whole vocabulary exists for intermediate elements that are neither clearly indoors nor outdoors, and which serve as natural links between the two, including *nokishita* (under the eaves), *nure-en* (veranda), and *watari rōka* (open corridor between wings). Even inside buildings, rooms are not entirely isolated from each other; remove the sliding room partitions and screens that separate them, and the result is a single, connected continuum.

The blurred distinction between a building's interior and exterior space reflects the Japanese belief that the human world is continuous with the world of nature. Nature is not seen as standing in opposition to humanity; on the contrary, the idea of humanity as an inseparable part of nature has been actively cultivated. Nor is it mere coincidence that Japanese art traditionally favored natural motifs like flowers, birds, and flowing water. Even the prominence of travel narratives in picture-scrolls and *michiyuki* (road-traveling) scenes in traditional Japanese theater presumably derives from the fact that travel unites people with nature.

Another noteworthy characteristic of the Japanese sense of beauty is the general absence of a concept of isolated "works of art" as such. Most artwork was connected with some element of daily life, and contributed to a certain world of beauty. Folding screens and sliding room partitions were not just media for paintings; they were also furniture. Hanging scrolls, too, were hung in the tokonoma alcove according to the season or on special occasions, establishing a space of beauty amid everyday life. This is also the reason for the often murky distinction between "art" and "craft" in the Western sense; many Japanese artists were also artisans, and the same motifs appeared in both paintings and craftworks.

Daily life in today's Japan has become highly Westernized, and traditional ways of living are gradually being lost. However, as long as the masterpieces of the past endure, so will the Japanese sense of beauty, and those masterpieces will continue to speak in a universal language to all those who love beauty in our world.

2. Object and Form

In October 1978, I paid my first visit to the Grand Shrine of Ise in some time. I was acting as guide for André Chastel, a professor of art history visiting from Paris—a former teacher of mine—and his wife.

Though a student of Western art history myself, when welcoming guests from outside Japan I am naturally expected to introduce my own country's culture to them. What's more, I must explain that culture using logic that makes sense to them. As a result, my visit to Ise spurred me to think comparatively about Japanese and Western culture, and this essay records one small part of those musings.

— 1 —

From a Western perspective, the most intriguing and in a sense mysterious thing about Ise Grand Shrine is the tradition of *sengū*, a complete rebuilding of the shrine that takes place once every twenty years. Or, if not the rebuilding itself, the fact that this tradition has survived so long, and the way of thinking that underlies it.

A single building—in this case, a single shrine—completely rebuilt, in exactly the same way, at regular intervals, for nearly thirteen hundred years. There is probably nothing to compare with this anywhere in the world, and certainly not in the West. And, since no culture is equipped with the logic to explain what does not exist within itself, Ise Grand Shrine cannot be explained through Western logic.

In short, the problem is this: Should the current shrine building be considered old, or new? In the context of Japanese architectural history, none would balk at treating Ise Grand Shrine as an example of ancient architecture, but in Western logical terms, for a building constructed in 1973 to be "ancient" is unthinkable. It is a twentieth-century building. If it transmits older styles, that only makes it a twentieth-century building made in the ancient manner.

Consider London's Palace of Westminster, where the Parliament of the United Kingdom meets. The current palace was rebuilt in the middle decades of the nineteenth century after the former palace burned down. The new structure was done in a medieval Gothic style, but no one considers it an example of medieval or Gothic architecture. On the contrary, it is a fine example of the nineteenth-century architectural style based on the Gothic. In books on the history of Western art and culture, the current Palace of Westminster appears in the nineteenth century, alongside, for example, the pre-Raphaelites. If we followed that logic in Japan, Ise Grand Shrine should be moved to the chapter on the twentieth century, beside abstract and pop art.

But there is more to Ise Grand Shrine than this logic may suggest. The Japanese have good reason for their inability to see the current shrine as a twentieth-century building. Specifically, although it was constructed in 1973, there is absolutely nothing of the twentieth century in it.

Sir Charles Barry, architect of the current Palace of Westminster, made a thorough study of the Gothic style and adopted it in all aspects of the new structure's design. Even so, every part of the building bears the stamp of the nineteenth century. Similarly, Notre-Dame de Paris, originally built in the thirteenth century, was the subject of a restoration and renovation project led by Eugène Viollet-le-Duc in the nineteenth century. At this time, the building was in such poor condition that it would have collapsed without some kind of intervention; in this sense, the project was a kind of *sengū*, too. Viollet-le-Duc was thoroughly familiar with Gothic architecture, and strove to restore the cathedral in the Gothic style. From our present-day perspective, however, the marks of his restoration are clearly distinguishable. The current cathedral of Notre-Dame is obviously a thirteenth-century building with nineteenth-century restorations and additions.

In short, architecture in the West is clearly identifiable with the time of its actual construction. Even extensions to a given building over the centuries reflect the respective ages in which they were added. Chartres Cathedral is an excellent example of this. A visitor standing before its western façade can clearly distinguish the Romanesque style of the lower part of the structure from the Gothic spire: the flow of time, visibly fixed in space.

From the Western perspective, one presumes, this is simply how history works. Western art history certainly rests on such assumptions. But the Grand Shrine at Ise, despite having been rebuilt sixty times, has never once borne the stamp of the age in which it was reconstructed. Every single time, it was rebuilt to be absolutely identical, literally "down to the inch." In the West, the notion of creating a building that is identical to an earlier one does not exist. Even when structures are lost to fire and rebuilt, the mark of the rebuilding is always visible. This makes it baffling, even unthinkable, that a shrine built in the twentieth century could be a famous example of "ancient architecture." In this sense, Ise Grand Shrine could be called a provocation directed at the logic of Western history itself.

This is not the only problem raised by the concept of *sengū*. Suppose that a capricious millionaire were to decide, right now, to build an identical copy of a still-extant ancient building. Indeed, projects not entirely dissimilar from this have in fact been undertaken in the United States. If we broaden the scope of the thought experiment to include not only the high drama of architecture but also crafts, paintings, and sculpture, we can identify many such projects, undertaken for a variety of reasons. In every one of those cases, however, even if the newly created object is identical to the original "down to the inch," it remains a copy, an imitation, a replica, or (when malice is intended) even a counterfeit, distinguished from the original as a matter of course. Even if the original is lost, the copy remains no more than a copy, the counterfeit merely a counterfeit; the idea that either could replace an original is absurd.

The Musée national des Monuments français in Trocadéro, Paris, houses a trove of plaster casts of medieval and Renaissance murals and sculptures, all accurate to the slightest detail. Murals surviving from the Romanesque age are often in dim, inaccessible locations, viewable only under confining restrictions even to those who make the effort to visit them in situ—but in this museum, visitors can admire them to their heart's content under ideal conditions. Some of the museum's holdings are reportedly copies of originals that are at risk of being lost forever due to the deterioration of the churches that house them. If those churches should fall, the copies in the museum will survive as unique and priceless testaments to the ways of the past. But however valuable the museum's holdings are as records, materials for study, and educational tools, they will never be as valuable as the lost originals—the "real thing." They will always be known as twentieth-century copies.

At Ise, however, the copy *does* replace the real thing—or, more accurately, the copy *is* the original, however absurd this may sound to the Western ear. The custom of rebuilding the entire shrine presumably began as an alternative solution when the first shrine grew old and needed repairs, but this should not be interpreted as "making do" with a copy when the real thing becomes damaged. The moment each new shrine is complete, it becomes the real thing.

The thinking behind the Musée national des Monuments français is the same as that of someone who stows a precious piece of heirloom jewelry in their safe and wears a replica instead. No matter how accurate that replica is, its value at the jeweler's will only ever be that of a replica. Even if the original is lost to some misfortune, its owner cannot insist that the replica has replaced it.

In the case of Ise Grand Shrine, however, a superficially similar position holding that the replica (although whether this word is even appropriate here is a major question) *is* the real thing has been accepted for over a thousand years. This is a powerful challenge to Western modes of thought about the essence of things and the essence of value.

— 2 —

The issue is not, of course, limited to Ise Grand Shrine. The survival of the shrine from antiquity to our own times in a manner that baffles Western logic is connected to the nature and values of the Japanese people—in short, to the way they see *things*, quite literally.

To begin with, the Japanese clearly do not value the *thing itself* as highly as Westerners. Alternatively, we might say that they do not feel that the thing itself contains the *essence* of the thing. What matters at Ise Grand Shrine is not the building itself. The building is important, of course, but that importance is not necessarily connected to any specific assemblage of construction materials. Even though it was constructed in the twentieth century, not to mention torn down and rebuilt countless times in the intervening centuries, the current Ise Grand Shrine has exactly the same value to the Japanese people as the building that stood there over a thousand years ago. Conversely, the Palace of Westminster will never be viewed as a structure of the Gothic era, no matter how faithfully its architect adopted the Gothic style. Its architectural value is as an example not of the Gothic style but of nineteenth-century architecture—specifically, the Gothic Revival. The current palace is inextricably bound to the historical moment of the mid-nineteenth century. It cannot escape those temporal limitations because it bears the unmistakable stamp of that age. Even if the palace, or any other nineteenth-century building, had been constructed as an exact replica of an existing Gothic structure—although such a thing would be unthinkable in the West—it would not be considered an example of the Gothic style, but only a trite imitation. This is because the collection of materials that constitutes the palace—its materiality—is not Gothic but nineteenth-century.

Under the same logic, the Grand Shrine at Ise should also be considered an imitation. And yet, despite being rebuilt every twenty years, the current structure is always accepted by the Japanese as the "real thing." We must conclude that what makes it genuine is not its materiality—or, at least, not only that—but some other factor that goes beyond materiality. What this might be is difficult to say, but our search for appropriate language tends to lead to words like *spirit* or *heart* or *soul*.

Naturally, I do not mean to argue for a simplistic worldview in which the West is "materialistic" while Japan is "spiritual." Western architecture, too, has a profound spiritual aspect, while the Ise Grand Shrine could not function as a shrine without material existence. However, notwithstanding this caveat, it does seem fair to say that spirituality in the West is difficult to separate from individual objects or beings, while in Japan materiality is not seen as having the same importance.

This fact corresponds more or less accurately to the differences between Western and Japanese conceptions of body and soul, or spirit and flesh. Some variety of dualism—that is, the division of human existence into body and soul—is likely universal, but on the question of which is more important, nations and peoples clearly differ. The Japanese traditionally emphasized the soul. Inokuchi Shōji's book *Nihon no sōshiki* (Funerary rituals in Japan, Hayakawa Shobō, 1965) states:

> Generally speaking, there are peoples who esteem and preserve dead bodies and those who discard the corpse and worship only the spirit within. Japan belongs to the latter category. . . . In ancient [Japanese] funeral rites, the body was considered impure, to be abandoned in the mountains or by the sea without looking back. Only the purified soul was considered worthy of worship as an ancestral spirit.

This worldview remains substantially unchanged to the present day. Bodies are no longer "abandoned . . . without looking back," of course, but Japanese ancestor veneration is still directed at spirits, not bodies. The flesh dies and passes away, and this is of no concern.

In the West, or at least the Christian world, the passing away of the flesh is problematic. Because Christianity teaches that the dead will rise from their graves for the Last Judgment, the body must be preserved until the last day of the world in a way that maintains individual identity. If the soul were assimilated to the ancestral spirits after the flesh was lost, as in Japan, it would not be able to receive its final judgment.

The ancient Egyptians—who, like the ancient Japanese, practiced an animistic faith centered around sun worship—famously believed that the spirit would need its flesh in the afterlife, and put great effort into ensuring the latter's preservation. In this respect, at least, the Western way of thinking about such matters resembles that of the ancient Egyptians. Western cultures did not create mummies, of course, and they knew that bodies decomposed in the earth leaving only bones. Even so, those bones had to be preserved with care so that they could be resurrected on Judgment Day and regain their flesh once more.

Many paintings of the Last Judgment show the dead rising from their graves, including the well-known frescos by Luca Signorelli in Orvieto Cathedral and Michelangelo in the Sistine Chapel. Interestingly enough, figures still emerging from the earth are depicted as skeletons, but those who have already gotten to their feet have their complete, original human forms. The logic is clear: identity is preserved in the materiality of the human body, even when it is reduced to bones. Individual souls are forever linked to individual bodies.

Nor can these ideas be dismissed as something from the distant past. In 1894, a project was launched to restore St. John's Church in Leipzig. The composer Johann Sebastian Bach was said to be buried in this church—specifically, by the southern wall, which was to be demolished in the renovations. This was seen as a good opportunity to create a new grave for Bach, but a problem arose: three coffins were unearthed, and no one knew which was his. (By that point, of course, none of them contained anything but bleached skeletons.) So, an investigative commission was formed with a professor of anatomy at its center. Under his direction, a sculptor named Carl Seffner added clay to a model of one of the exhumed skulls to show how its owner must have looked in life—literally "resurrecting" him from a skeletal state. Seffner's work was compared to portraits of Bach made during his lifetime, the committee formally identified these remains as Bach's, and the bones were reinterred in a new grave.

Graves are sometimes moved in Japan, too, for any number of reasons. The necessary rituals are performed in such cases, but it is unlikely that anyone would bother to investigate bones of uncertain identity from more than a century ago. This is because the object of veneration for the Japanese is the soul of the deceased. In the West, however, even if Bach's soul is venerated, it must be together with Bach's body—and nobody else's.

When I spoke on this topic on one occasion in the past, an audience member raised an objection: in the case of a plane crash or accident in the mountains, do the Japanese not consider recovery of the bodies to be the highest priority, to be accomplished at any cost? Do not surviving family members plead to receive part of the remains, even if only a fragment? Does this not represent a similar attachment to the materiality of the body?

It is true that the bodies of the dead are handled with greater care in today's Japan than they once were, and cutting-edge DNA testing and various other methods are used to ascertain who unidentified remains belong to. Nevertheless, the Japanese attachment to bones and other remains still strikes me as different in character from that seen in the West. Japanese families plead to receive even the slightest fragment of bone not because they believe that fragment *is* the dead person in some sense, but because they need it as a means to remember that person. Accordingly, when remains are tragically unrecoverable, something that the person used to wear or carry can fill the same role: a cap, or even a bag. In the West, Bach's skull is thought to *be* Bach, but in Japan, remains are more like a memento, which is a function that other objects can perform equally well.

The Japanese word for "memento" in this sense is *katami*. Etymologically, it is related to the word *kata*, "form," which is highly interesting in itself. If the West has a philosophy of things or objects (*mono*), Japan has a philosophy of forms (*kata*) arising from a tendency to view forms or shapes (*katachi*) as more important than things themselves. Each time the Grand Shrine at Ise is rebuilt, it becomes an entirely new *thing*, but its value remains unchanged because it inherits the original, unchanged *form*.

— 3 —

These values are also evident in Japanese life outside the religious sphere. One obvious example is the culture of name succession in kabuki.

Stage names like "Danjūrō" and "Utaemon" have been passed down to many succeeding generations of kabuki actors, but the value attached to them remains unchanged, just as the Grand Shrine at Ise remains the Grand Shrine no matter how many times it is rebuilt. In centuries past, names were passed down by warriors and merchants in much the same way. The West has some superficially similar practices, such as "numbered" kings like Henri IV and Louis XVI, but these are simply rulers who happen to share the same name. The names themselves, "Henri" or "Louis," do not have a special meaning or value. This is not the case for a name like "Danjūrō," which possesses a kind of character and value, almost like a persona in itself. Indeed, this is the entire point of name succession. If "Danjūrō" were merely an arrangement of letters, like "Louis" or "Henri," there would be no need for actors to "inherit" it. Each Danjūrō is a separate person, of course, but when they succeed to the name, they adopt the same "Danjūrō" persona. A value transcending that of any individual is transmitted from one actor to the next, each of whom inherits it faithfully. Name succession is thus highly similar to the *sengū* of Ise Grand Shrine.

In this respect, succeeding to a name means adopting a new persona. It would not do for a newly created Danjūrō to behave just as he did as Ebizō yesterday. Succeeding to the name indicates at least his willingness to strive to cast off Ebizō and become Danjūrō, and those around him expect nothing less. "Danjūrō" becomes a kind of role that the individual must play in his private life. The "role awareness" (*yakuwari ishiki*) often noted as an element of the Japanese character by those who know the culture well may trace its original form to this practice. A role is, after all, another kind of form, or *kata*.

"Although my opinion as an individual is otherwise, given my position I am forced to say . . ." This is a highly Japanese way of speaking, interpreted in the West as at best incomprehensible and at worst sly and duplicitous. It is viewed as untrue to both the individual and the role. However, few Japanese people would see any mystery in a speaker's opinions—at least, those they express in public—changing with their position. A position is a kind of role, and to speak in accordance with one's role is only natural. Japanese people tend to avoid switching companies, and frown on those who do, but they show no great resistance to switching roles within a company. An employee who was in charge of human resources yesterday might be assigned to the factory floor today. Some changes are even more extreme, such as the chair of the union committee suddenly being appointed to a labor management position. In a case like this, the same person who yesterday insisted on the necessity of raising wages will today argue for suppressing them, and no one will think it suspicious or unnatural. The employee has "succeeded to" the name "labor management director" and become a different person as a result.

This way of thinking is difficult for some Westerners to understand. To return to the previous architectural metaphor, just as a Western building's value is inseparably linked to its materiality, so the Western individual is linked to their role. This difference in perspective explains why the Japanese have sometimes been described as untrustworthy.

I have read that, shortly after the end of the Second World War, the Allied Occupation wanted to stop people playing the game of shogi, which it deemed too militaristic. When shogi players objected, pointing out that Westerners played chess, the responsible GHQ officer insisted that shogi was much worse than chess, for two reasons. First, chess has both a king and a queen, indicating equal rights for men and women, but shogi only has a king—a feudal state of affairs. Second, captured pieces in shogi come under the control of the capturing player and attack their former comrades—an immoral endorsement of treachery. Whether this story is true I cannot say, but even if it is completely fictional, it is an intriguing encapsulation of the Western viewpoint.

Chess and shogi, of course, derive from the same Indian source, although the latter passed through China on its way to Japan. Throughout this family of games, the fundamental principles are the same, but each country has its own variation on the types of pieces used, as well as their numbers and abilities. For example, the queen appears only in chess; it is fair to call her characteristic of the West. Conversely, the shogi rule allowing reuse of captured pieces is not found in the original Indian game or even its Chinese descendent: it is completely unique to Japan. It seems reasonable to interpret this as a manifestation of Japanese "role awareness," which the West has such difficulty understanding.

Professor Chastel happened to love chess, and on the way home I explained the rules of shogi to him. Unsurprisingly, the hardest part for him to grasp was the notion of reusing captured pieces. When I explained this rule, the surprise on his face was utterly genuine—just as it was when I had explained that the Grand Shrine, a masterpiece of ancient architecture, had been erected only five years earlier.

3. Forms of Seeing, East and West

On "Naturalness" in *Portrait of Chin-Jung* and *Portrait of Philibert Rivière*

Whenever I see Yasui Sōtarō's 1934 *Portrait of Chin-Jung* in Tokyo's National Museum of Modern Art, I am seized by a strange feeling. Putting that feeling into words is difficult, but, if pressed, I might call it a kind of unease. Despite the painting's utterly stable, poised composition, something in it will not allow the viewer to relax. Or perhaps we might more accurately say that it will not allow the viewer to accept what they see. At first glance, the subject of the portrait, a woman in a close-fitting blue Chinese dress, sits calmly in an armchair, looking utterly at ease. On closer inspection, however, her pose is actually quite awkward.

To understand why, an apt comparison is Jean-Auguste-Dominique Ingres's *Portrait of Philibert Rivière*, painted in the early nineteenth century. Ingres's portrait also depicts its subject in an armchair from a slight angle. The subjects of the two paintings face in opposite directions, but their poses share many common elements: both sit casually in a chair, legs crossed, arm on the armrest nearest the viewer.

I do not mean to suggest that *Portrait of Chin-Jung* might derive directly from *Portrait of Philibert Rivière*. Yasui spent seven years in France, from 1907 to 1914, so he undoubtedly saw Ingres's work, but there is no reason to suppose that he had this particular portrait in mind when he painted *Chin-Jung* twenty years after returning to Japan. The similarity of the pose does not suggest direct influence; a slight angle is simply the most convenient perspective from which to depict a subject in an armchair, as countless other slightly angled portraits attest. Indeed, it is precisely because the pose is so unremarkable that a comparison of the two paintings reveals differences in how these two individuals—one Japanese, one French—saw the world.

Jean-Auguste-Dominique Ingres, *Portrait of Philibert Rivière (Monsieur Philibert Rivière)*. Musée du Louvre, Paris. Photo © RMN-Grand Palais (Musée du Louvre) / Franck Raux / Distributed by AMF-DNPartcom

Yasui Sōtarō, *Portrait of Chin-Jung (Kin'yō)*. National Museum of Modern Art, Tokyo. Photo: MOMAT / DNPartcom

One immediately obvious feature of Ingres's portrait is the "naturalness" of its representation. Ingres constantly exhorted his pupils to "Make nature your teacher," and the "naturalness" we see here has no particular grounding in abstract aesthetics. We might more simply and frankly call it traditional realism: re-creating a three-dimensional presence on the canvas as faithfully as possible. Everything in the painting is depicted so as to convey the presence of a real body behind it: not just the visible parts of Rivière himself, like his face and right hand, but also the clothing he wears, right down to the meticulously painted wrinkles and folds. Nor is this inconsistent with the fact that Ingres's style differs greatly from the work of later artists like Courbet, the leader of what art history would call the Realist movement in the nineteenth century. Ingres was well practiced in the techniques of traditional Academism, but his visual world does not fit neatly within the Academic frame. Even in this early portrait, painted before Ingres went to Italy, the books and prints on the table to the right of the subject are meticulously drawn, but the spatial relationships within the work are far from clear. Given the position of the chair and its angle in relation to the viewer, it does not extend far enough into the background. Combined with the near-featureless wall that serves as backdrop, this distinctive style of representation dramatically compresses the space of the picture, even leveling it. We might not call it "flattened" as such, but the "thinness" of space in Ingres's work is so evident that some critics consider it an essential characteristic of his style.

However, despite this all but instinctive tendency toward "leveled," "thin" spaces, Ingres's Rivière resolutely exists as a physical body. Put another way, it is Rivière himself who guarantees the three-dimensionality of the space despite its extreme thinness overall. As viewers, we see him as an individual occupying the place he would if the space were real, and the slight angle he sits at convinces us that sufficient space is indeed represented within the picture. This is what I mean by the "naturalness" of this portrait.

However, "naturalness" in this sense is almost entirely absent from Yasui's *Portrait of Chin-Jung*. Because the painting depicts a person sitting at a slight angle in an armchair, we expect from it a spatial representation corresponding to the real place occupied by the model. Unlike *Philibert Rivière*, which meets that expectation almost completely, *Chin-Jung* meets it only in the subject's face. From the neck down, we have no clear idea what sort of space the body concealed within the clothing occupies. Or rather, we have a general idea, but it does not fully correspond to what we would naturally expect from the model's pose.

When Yasui's *Portrait of Chin-Jung* and *Portrait of Professor Tamamushi* were shown at the 1934 Nika exhibition, Kojima Kikuo called them "original enough to display to all the world . . . unprecedented . . . contemporary portraits without precedent in Japan." Even so, he criticized *Chin-Jung* on the grounds that "the thighs could be a little thicker" (Kamon Yasuo, *Yasui Sōtarō*, Kōdansha, 1962; Vol. 6 of *Nihon Kindai kaiga zenshū* [Collected modern Japanese paintings]).

In a portrait of a subject seated at an angle, the thighs extend into the foreground, toward the viewer; their representation secures the depth of

Jean-Auguste-Dominique Ingres, *Portrait of Baronne de Rothschild.*

the depicted space and is an important element in conveying fullness of body. In Ingres's portrait, the thighs in their white breeches are a striking point of expression; one might argue that painters prefer to depict seated subjects at a slight angle rather than frontally or in profile for precisely this reason. However, as Kojima observes, this normally crucial element is hardly brought to life at all in *Chin-Jung*. Underneath the model's blue clothing, the structure and pose of the model's lower body, from waist to knee, is difficult to discern from the painting alone. Furthermore, the unclear position of her thighs makes it impossible to tell from the folds in her clothing how her legs are crossed. If not for the ankle and foot visible beneath the hem at bottom left, we might even conclude that her thighs were crossed the opposite way.

We might be tempted to attribute this to the fact that Rivière is wearing breeches while Chin-Jung is in Chinese attire, but this is not a sufficient explanation. Ingres's portrait of Baronne de Rothschild depicts the subject in a much fuller skirt while still making clear how her legs are crossed. In *Chin-Jung*, the anatomical vagueness of the subject's lower body is undeniable, and this is surely not unrelated to the fact that, compared to *Rivière*, too much of the chair's seat is unoccupied on the side facing us—the model seems to be oddly positioned off to one side.

However, an even stranger aspect of *Chin-Jung* is the depiction of the subject's upper body, particularly the shoulders. The subject is seen from the same angle as the chair she sits in; for this reason, her face is depicted in three-quarter profile, and as a result, her upper body usually would be, too. We might also have expected what is perhaps the most common pose in portraiture: the body at an angle, and the face turned slightly toward the viewer, indicating the subject's awareness of the painter's presence. This, indeed, is what we see in *Philibert Rivière*. In *Chin-Jung*, however, the face maintains the same angle as the chair, as if the subject is entirely unaware of the painter (and, by extension, the viewers—us), but her upper body *is* depicted as if slightly turned toward us. The right shoulder—the one further from us—is particularly emphasized, so that while the subject seems to be sitting quietly in a chair, she is actually twisting her torso and thrusting her shoulders out. What is more, her *lower* body appears to turn back to the side again, so that everything from the hips down is twisted. This is a highly unnatural way to sit. Given an armchair, mimicking Rivière's pose would be a simple matter, but re-creating Chin-Jung's would be quite a challenge.

In principle, when a subject is painted from an angle, the shoulder nearest the viewer should be larger and more noticeable than the more distant one. The logic of perspective dictates this, as does our own intuition. *Philibert Rivière* is drawn in exactly this way, imparting an impression of "naturalness" to the viewer. However, *Chin-Jung* is just the opposite: the distant shoulder is the larger, more eye-catching one. This is "unnatural" in itself. It leaves the shoulders and upper body pointed in a different direction than the face, and makes the connection to the head somewhat awkward. In the context of traditional Academism, such a depiction would be dismissed as immature drafting.

But this dismissal will not work on Yasui. After arriving in France in 1907, he spent three years under Jean-Paul Laurens at the Académie Julian receiving thorough training in the fundamentals of figurative art. Moreover, he almost always won at least one prize in the monthly oil painting and sketching competitions held in Laurens's classroom from October to February each year—a testament to the prodigious drafting skill he attained under Laurens. In a letter to his older brother Motoshichi on March 10, 1910, Yasui listed his achievements in the contests that season: a 50-franc prize in the male full-body oil portraiture category in October, a prize in oils and drawing in November, oils in January, and oils and drawing again in February. Laurens's atelier was well known for giving pupils a thorough ground-ing in Academic fundamentals, so Yasui's outstanding success there indicates that his grasp of traditional Western painting technique was more than adequate. In another letter to Motoshichi, dated December 12, 1909, Yasui says, "Winning a prize at the Julian is no great honor. Or even at École nationale supérieure des beaux-arts. They are nothing but hapless daubers." If these words show great self-confidence, it was by no means unjustified.

Clearly, then, Yasui was perfectly capable of painting *Chin-Jung* using the same traditional techniques as Ingres, had he so desired. If he chose to ignore Western traditions of representation, he must have had a reason to do so. In fact, "ignore" is not strong enough a word—the portrait intentionally flouts traditional standards, as a comparison of the subject's two shoulders makes evident. Overall, forms in the painting are clear, with crisp outlines, but at the subject's left shoulder—the one closer to us—the manner of representa-tion becomes much vaguer. This, undoubtedly, is where Yasui struggled the most. In this part of the painting, and nowhere else, the plain, pared-down background is drawn with extremely rough strokes that even bleed into the subject's clothing. It feels as if Yasui is intentionally trying to undermine the effect of what would otherwise be a clear field of dark blue. Meanwhile, the model's right shoulder—the one further from us—is not just larger and more noticeable, it is even limned by a white outline to emphasize its presence.

This white outline is the most logically inexplicable part of the painting. Yes, the blue dress worn by the model has a white floral motif—but the motif is always round, and there is no sign of anything like the continuous white line on the subject's right shoulder. Similarly, the white embroidery that adorns the dress's hem and collar has no reason to appear on the shoulder too. If the white line was not part of the subject being depicted, but Yasui includ-ed it anyway, his purpose could only be creative—to separate the color fields in the painting, like Gauguin often did during one period. In short, Yasui added the outline to emphasize the shoulder's presence. If this seems odd, that is because it is. Despite his mastery of traditional Western Academic drafting techniques, Yasui intentionally flouted them by de-emphasizing the near shoulder and reinforcing the far one. The question, then, is why he would do this.

Japanese and Western Forms of Seeing

At this point, I must make something clear. My intention in comparing the portraits by Yasui and Ingres and analyzing their differences is not to declare one superior to the other. I observed that "naturalness" is a key characteristic of Ingres's work, but "naturalness" does not determine a painting's value, and it is not "naturalness" alone that makes *Portrait of Philibert Rivière* a masterpiece. My point is simply this: while the "naturalness" of Ingres's portrait involves one particular way of seeing—one that formed the foundation of Western art for over four hundred years, beginning in the Renaissance—*Portrait of Chin-Jung* is based on a different way of seeing entirely.

To borrow the terminology of Swiss art historian Heinrich Wölfflin, the difference is a matter of *Sehformen*: "forms of seeing." Every age and every nation has its own unique forms of seeing, and these have no direct connection to artistic or creative value. Obviously, even among artworks based on the same form of seeing, some will be of interest and others will not.

I called the connection in *Chin-Jung* between the head facing one direction and the body facing another "awkward." We might say exactly the same thing about the human figures in ancient Egyptian murals, whose heads are depicted in profile while their torsos face forward. Here, too, the issue is not the creative value of Egyptian murals but the form of seeing of the ancient Egyptians. In exactly the same way, we must keep in mind that the form of seeing in Japanese painter Yasui Sōtarō's *Chin-Jung* differs from that in Ingres's work, which is based on traditional Western Academism.

I am fond of *Portrait of Chin-Jung* as an individual work of art. It is undeniably one of the high points in Yasui's long artistic career. However, this also makes it one of the end points of modern Western-style art in Japan. Yasui was not an ancient Egyptian but a Japanese artist, and one who labored mightily to introduce Western artistic expression to Japan. This was a man who went to France to "acquire" Western art and mastered its traditional techniques so completely that he startled even the French painters who were his rivals. Irresistibly drawn as I am to the refreshing charm of the painting, it would not do for me to forget that truth. *Portrait of Chin-Jung* was painted nearly seventy years after the Meiji Restoration of 1868. Since serious efforts to learn Western painting techniques began even before that, in the late Edo period, the passion for "acquiring" the art of the West had been burning in Japanese artists for over a century by the time Yasui created this work. *Portrait of Chin-Jung* is one outcome of these long, unstinting efforts, a fact which I never fail to find shocking, in its way. The sense of unease I mentioned at the beginning of this essay is not, of course, unrelated to this shock.

Another question it behooves us to ask when considering the forms of seeing in Yasui's and Ingres's work is the degree to which these differences can be attributed to a simple Japan–West dichotomy. Ingres's portrait was painted in the early nineteenth century, Yasui's in the 1930s. As Wölfflin himself stressed, while forms of seeing differ between nations, they also change with the times. We cannot entirely ignore the 130 years that separate the two works—especially since those 130 years neatly encompass a vast upheaval in Western artistic practice, from Impressionism to Cubism. The Impressionists, and particularly Cézanne, changed the whole course of Western art. If "naturalness" was the fundamental grammar of creative language in Ingres's time, the language of the twentieth century made deformation its idiom instead. Nevertheless, notwithstanding the vast gap between Ingres and Cézanne, I truly feel that an even wider gulf exists between the two of them and Yasui.

Certainly, during his time in France, Yasui was strongly influenced by the Impressionists, and particularly by Pissarro. But whether Cézanne's influence on Yasui was identical in essence to his influence on the Fauves and the Cubists is another matter entirely. Yasui arrived in 1907, the year after Cézanne's death; at the urging of sculptor Ogiwara Morie (Rokuzan), he visited a major Cézanne retrospective held at the Salon d'automne that year— but, in his own words, he "didn't really understand it." It would be some time before his interest in Cézanne deepened. For a young Japanese painter newly arrived in Paris, this is not surprising, but it does show that whatever Cézanne meant for Yasui's art, it was not the same as the role he played for European artists of Yasui's generation.

To be frank, while Cézanne's "influence" is often cited in discussions of Yasui's art, I myself do not think it so essential. I do not mean to say, of course, that Yasui learned nothing from the sublime achievements of the man who painted the *Mont Sainte-Victoire* series. From a young age, Yasui was blessed with both a rich artistic sensitivity and a high capacity for intellectual understanding, and we can easily imagine him being drawn to Cézanne's work. Still, I believe that the lessons he learned from that work were completely different from those learned by the Cubists and the Fauves—just as Van Gogh and Gauguin learned things from Japanese ukiyo-e prints that Japanese artists of the time would never have imagined.

Note, too, that Cézanne, like many of the great "revolutionaries" in Western art history, was highly faithful to tradition. To see his work hanging in Bouguereau's salon was the great hope of his life, and, even as Impressionism opened his eyes to new worlds of color, he sought to "redo Poussin," a painter of the French Baroque who lived from 1594 to 1665. Like his fellow "revolutionary" Manet, Cézanne considered himself a traditionalist. He fully sensed the weight of his tradition, cultivated over a long history, and did his utmost to inherit it faithfully. We might even say that this is what enabled him to become a revolutionary.

Here we must touch on the essential structure of Western culture. In the West, history undergoes a process of internal foment, first denying its past and then absorbing it to become something fresh and new. In Japan, however, revolution always comes from without. Like contact between volatile chemicals, the process involves the combustion and confusion of violent energies, but when the agitation subsides, the result is the addition of something new *from the outside world*. Older presences are not immune to the influence of these new arrivals, of course, but the old does not become the new the way a caterpillar becomes a butterfly. The past remains alive. This is why, while Western art history can be viewed as an account of the *development* of forms, art history in Japan must recognize the *parallel existence* of a variety of forms. In Europe, Gothic forms were born within and developed from Romanesque forms; by the time every city was erecting its own Gothic cathedral, no one was building in the Romanesque style. In Japan, however, the arrival in the medieval period of a new "Chinese-style" (*karayō*) architecture (also known as *Zenshūyō* or "Zen style") did not mark the end of existing traditions. In the same way, when Western painting and music reached Japan in the Meiji era, local artistic traditions were not abandoned (notwithstanding a short period of confusion). On the contrary, Western painting served to sharpen the outlines of Japanese painting by virtue of contrast. To this day, "Western-style" and "Japanese-style" painting are practiced in Japan side-by-side, just like their musical equivalents.

This illustrates a great difference between Japan and the West in how external influences exist in the cultural sphere, and the nature of their effects. If we were to prepare a "balance sheet" for the century and more of cultural negotiations between East and West since the Meiji Restoration, it would obviously show a severe "trade deficit" for Japan. And, indeed, the presence and meaning of Western culture in Japan vastly outweighs that of Japanese culture in the West. Japan may have recorded a relatively large number of "exports" in the fields of painting, printmaking, and other visual arts, but even there, the influence of ukiyo-e and *nihonga* (traditional Japanese painting) on the West was minor compared to the influx of Western art into Japan. Countless Japanese travelers went to Europe to learn Western painting in the Meiji period and after, but not a single Western painter made the opposite voyage to learn ukiyo-e or *nihonga* in Japan. Or, at least, no painter who played an important role in Western art history. Oddly, however, notwithstanding this adverse "trade balance," the overwhelming influence of Western art never posed an existential threat to *nihonga* in Japan, but the sporadic and episodic influence of ukiyo-e changed the very course of painting in the West. Given that ukiyo-e spurred Western painters to completely disavow what had come before, if we measure by results rather than number of artists or amount of knowledge exchanged, we might find that ukiyo-e had by far the larger impact.

My goal here is not, of course, to amend some imaginary balance sheet and put Japan in the black. But "influence" can be considered in both quantitative and qualitative terms, and these qualitative aspects may contain a clue to an essential difference between Japanese and Western culture. The arrival of Western art bestowed something new on Japan, but the nation did not disavow its older art; by contrast, the influence of ukiyo-e became a catalyst for transforming the old Western art *into* something new. If anything, the fact that this coexists with a starkly reversed disparity of influence in quantitative terms only throws the problem's essence into sharper relief.

Ukiyo-e alone did not cause the transformation in Western art, of course. This much is clear from the evidently sporadic influence it had. The energy of change, of revolution, came from within Western art itself. Ukiyo-e simply pressed the launch button, as it were. It need not even have been ukiyo-e. Had Japan's "isolation" lasted a hundred more years, Western-style painting might not have found a foothold there, but sooner or later the European art world would have birthed a Cézanne. Just as Ingres was influenced by Raphael despite not being a Renaissance painter himself, Cézanne is clearly connected by tradition to Ingres across the gulf of years.

Accordingly, it is not surprising that what the painter of *Portrait of Chin-Jung* received from Cézanne at a young age differed from what Picasso and Matisse learned from the same Cézanne in the context of Western art history. To Yasui, in all probability, Cézanne was first and foremost a *Western* painter, and his "Cézanne experience"—if he had something worthy of that phrase—was but another variation on his "Western experience."

This is not to accuse Yasui of failing to sufficiently understand Cézanne. I doubt that any Japanese painter interpreted Cézanne the way the Fauves or Cubists did. In 1915, one year after Yasui returned to Japan, he exhibited over forty works he had painted in Europe, in a special section of the second Nika Exhibition, held at Mitsukoshi Department Store in Tokyo. Coincidentally, the young painters of Japan were intensely interested in Cézanne at that time, partly due to an article in *Shirakaba* (White birch) magazine introducing the artist, and Yasui's Western style was generally understood as connected to Cézanne's. The immediate and significant effect this had on Japan's eager young artists is clear from Yamawaki Shintoku's review of the fourth Nika Exhibition held two years later. Writing in the October 1917 issue of *Chūō bijutsu* (Central art), Shintoku's sharp critical eye divided the exhibited works into three groups: Cézanne-like, Cubist and Futurist, and Sōdosha-style (referring to a group led by Kishida Ryūsei). The Cézanne-like works were the most numerous; furthermore, as Shintoku shrewdly observed in the same review, the name was something of a misnomer. "Rather than Cézanne's style, it might more accurately be called Yasui's style. It is a style made up of flat masses, rectilinear outlines, and dark colors, as seen in Yasui's landscapes (if not initially his nudes) upon his return to Japan and for some time thereafter." Indeed, the "flat masses" and "rectilinear outlines" in Yasui's work owe more to Japanese forms of seeing than they do to Cézanne, and the "dark colors" are those of traditional Western Academism, as represented by Laurens and others Yasui studied with in Paris. The subsequent development of Yasui's art banished those dark colors in favor of brighter hues, in a turn toward an even more thoroughly Japanese style. *Portrait of Chin-Jung* is, of course, an extension of this.

If we examine Cézanne's portraits of subjects in chairs angled the same way, we find within all of them a form of seeing much closer to *Philibert Rivière* than *Chin-Jung*, notwithstanding the temporal separation between Cézanne and Ingres. *Madame Cézanne with a Fan*, owned by a private collector in Switzerland, is an excellent example. In place of another laborious comparison of details, suffice it to note the most distinctive aspect: the subject's shoulders. Cézanne, exactly like Ingres, makes his model's right shoulder—the one closer to us—larger and more noticeable than the other, seeking to re-create within the picture the depth of an actual body. This is the exact opposite of Yasui's approach in *Chin-Jung* of enlarging the more distant shoulder in order to process the image by means of "flat masses." Accordingly, Madame Cézanne's pose has none of the unnatural twistedness

Paul Cézanne, *Madame Cézanne with a Fan (Madame Cézanne à l'éventail)*. Emil Bührle Collection, Zürich. Photo: Bridgeman Images / DNPartcom

Itō Shinsui, *Portrait of Mrs. N (Enu-shi Fujin-zō)*.

of Chin-Jung's, and looks as natural to us as Monsieur Rivière's.

That Cézanne, despite his "revolutionary" explorations, shared a fundamental form of seeing with Ingres speaks to how firmly rooted these forms have been in the West since the Renaissance. In the same way, the fact that Yasui, whose mastery of Western technique was so assured that he won monthly prizes at the Académie Julian, nevertheless returned to the "flat mass" in *Chin-Jung* reveals the stubborn persistence within him of Japanese forms of seeing. *Chin-Jung's* fellows in representational terms can be found not among portraiture by Cézanne or Ingres but in the world of Japanese art, upholding the traditional techniques of Japan—for example, in Itō Shinsui's 1953 *Portrait of Mrs. N*. In this work, too, the model's far shoulder is rather prominent, if not as much as Chin-Jung's. Furthermore, while in the portraits by Cézanne and Ingres the far shoulder is not only partly concealed by the body but also lower than the near one, in *Mrs. N* and *Chin-Jung* the far shoulder is actually *higher* than the other. Shinsui has posed his model rising slightly from the seat, and his perspective is also somewhat elevated.

Yasui Sōtarō, *Lamasery in Chengde*
(*Shōtoku no ramabyō*). Eisei Bunko.

While this skillful arrangement prevents her pose from seeming "twisted" like Chin-Jung's, the mode of representation clearly differs from that of Cézanne or Ingres. At the very least, Mrs. N's upper half is handled more "flatly" than Madame Cézanne's or Monsieur Rivière's.

This tendency toward flattening seen in *Portrait of Chin-Jung* is also readily apparent in Yasui's landscapes, as Shintoku observed in the review cited earlier. Yasui showed *Lamasery in Chengde* at the first Issuikai Exhibition in 1937, three years after unveiling *Chin-Jung*. Immediately lauded as a masterpiece and still counted among his finest work, *Chengde* is also an excellent example of his technique. Not only is the lamasery's façade depicted in frontal view using vivid pinks, greens, and yellows, in the bottom half of the picture, the intermediate space between the lamasery's entrance and the building itself is handled as a flat mass. The stone staircase curving in a great S at the center of this space gives the impression of a small hill, but nothing apart from that staircase suggests any depth at all. In fact, the opposite is true: the hill, painted chiefly in yellows and greens, looks like a kind of platform on which the lamasery has been placed. At the very least, we can say that Yasui's use of color emphasizes flatness over depth.

Comparing this to Cézanne's landscapes makes the point even clearer. The works in Cézanne's *Mont Sainte-Victoire* series, which he became particularly fond of painting in his later years, have basically the same compo-

Paul Cézanne, *Mont Sainte-Victoire.*
The Philadelphia Museum of Art / Art
Resource, NY / DNPartcom.

sition as *Chengde*: the painting's top half contains the towering mass of the mountain, and the bottom half the space between the painter and his subject. The actual distance between painter and subject was much greater in Cézanne's case, of course, but Cézanne strove mightily to realize on the canvas the sprawling nature of that space. He spent countless hours over countless days battling with his paints, Mont Sainte-Victoire before him, determined to re-create as faithfully as he could the mountain's sense of presence and the vast space below. In *Lamasery at Chengde*, by contrast, Yasui takes the building's façade and the slope before it as flat masses, challenging himself to impart as creative an order as possible to these subjects.

Spatial Expression and the Problem of Pictorial Autonomy

The extent to which Cézanne was drawn to the depth and space of reality, even as he pursued pictorial autonomy and creative order, is evident in his all-too-famous exhortation to "treat nature by means of the cylinder, sphere, and cone." These words, originally from a letter to his friend Emile Bernard, are generally understood to express what might be called Cézanne's "will to order," by which the endless diversity of existing things is reduced to geometric forms for use as structural elements in his work. Indeed, this interpretation is correct, and this was also the lesson the early Cubists took from Cézanne. But we should not overlook the fact that Cézanne's list of geometric forms does not include the cube. The cube is surely the simplest and most basic "geometric form," so Cézanne's exclusion of it from his list must have been intentional. Why would he embrace "the cylinder, sphere, and cone," but not the cube?

The main difference between the cube (or rectangular cuboid) and the other forms is that, depending on the perspective, the cube can present a flat face to the viewer. Yasui's *Lamasery in Chengde* treats the cuboid building in just this way, by means of its flat façade. The cylinder, sphere, and cone, however, have no flat façade. Whichever direction they are viewed from, their surface always flows away to the rear. This necessarily places them in a space with clear depth.

In fact, so long as the painter treats nature "by means of the cylinder, sphere, and cone," the image cannot be treated "flatly." In this respect, Ingres and Cézanne are similar. Where the two differ is how they represent that roundness. Ingres uses the traditional Western technique of shading, depicting shadows with darker colors; Cézanne's contact with the Impressionists taught him that "shadows" do not exist—or, more accurately, that a shadow is a color too—and so he uses coloristic expression instead. While he abandoned traditional methods of perspective and shading, he did not reject three-dimensional forms of seeing altogether.

When Japanese people first encountered Western pictorial expression in the Edo period, what astonished them most was its three-dimensionality. One story tells of Hiraga Gennai, one of the standard-bearers for the importation of new Western knowledge during the Tokugawa shogunate, visiting the painter Odano Naotake in Kakunodate, Akita, and asking him to draw a *kagami-mochi*—a kind of rice cake consisting of two discs on top of each other, the top one somewhat smaller like a snowman—from directly above. As the story goes, Naotake considered the request, then drew the picture as asked. Gennai criticized the result, pointing out that it could just as easily be a tray or a wheel, and then taught Naotake the technique of Western-style shading for the first time.

The point of the story is that in the Japanese approach to painting, where a circular outline was used to depict the subject's form, there was no way to represent the bulge at the center of the *kagami-mochi*—its three-dimensional roundness. This episode is part of Kakunodate's oral tradition, and I do not know how much of it is true, but, historical truth aside, there is little doubt that the painters of the Edo period were utterly astonished at Western techniques for representing a three-dimensional world. Indeed, in his *Seiyō gadan* (Discussion of Western art), Shiba Kōkan makes a very similar point about the impossibility of distinguishing a circle from a sphere using Eastern techniques, concluding that the Western methods that made this distinction possible were superior. Kōkan's views on this matter survived unchanged in the philosophy of Takahashi Yuichi, a Western-style painter of the late Edo period who respected Kōkan deeply. The following passage by Yuichi makes this clear:

> The art of Western nations has always esteemed realism [*shajitsu*]. The myriad things before our eyes being designs of the creator, faithful depictions of them are smaller, artificial creations of the brush. . . . Japanese and Chinese art begins from stylistic details and concludes with substantial details. Western art begins from substantial details and concludes with stylistic details. Stylistic details betray the object; substantial details preserve it. Stylistic details are depicted beginning from outlines; substantial details beginning from shading. To describe the masterful techniques of Western painting, it is like when the sun and moon shine in the vast darkness of space and clearly reveal every form, concave and convex, near and far, shallow and deep. Perceiving this, people [in the West] devised methods for artistic depiction. Their paintings therefore obey the "law of three faces" [differentiating convex, concave, and flat], and subjects are depicted as larger or smaller to distinguish near from far. Because these techniques are founded on the pursuit of rationality, for those who seek to approach the truth, arrive at the sublime, and impart life, it is realism that is esteemed, and its foundations lie in the application of shading.

Yuichi took up the brush to write these words while he was engaged at the Painting Bureau of the Kaiseijo, a shogunate-run institute for Western studies. In fact, he went so far as to post the full text on the bureau's wall. The full text, later reproduced in the privately published *Takahashi Yuichi rireki* (Personal history of Takahashi Yuichi), is a valuable historical document showing where Yuichi, one of the first to make a serious attempt at adopting Western painting techniques, saw the essential differences between "Japanese and Chinese" and "Western" painting.

Yuichi showed great artistic talent from a young age, learning formal technique as an apprentice to a painter of the Kanō school. He was fully conversant with "Japanese and Chinese art"; this familiarity, perhaps, was why "Western art" came as such a powerful shock to him. Little is known for certain about the specific Western artworks he encountered at that early stage, but it was clearly the techniques of perspective, modeling, and shading—that is, the means by which a Western artist could distinguish a *kagami-mochi* from a tray—that astonished him. These techniques were by that point conventional in the West, but this was exactly why Yuichi was able to grasp their effect from what were likely second- or third-rate imported works.

The effort Yuichi expended in learning Western painting techniques, the sheer passion, comes through with almost painful clarity in his work. He fervently sought to render each subject with a sense of reality. At the same time, it cannot be denied that the spatial relationships between subjects are not always clear—or, at least, not in the same way that they are in Western representations of space. This is particularly true in Yuichi's still lifes, where his raw fidelity to the images he depicts remains startling to this day. For example, in *Reader and Notebook* (*Tokuhon to sōshi*), in the collection of the Kotohiragū Shrine Museum in Kagawa Prefecture, the tiniest detail of every item is rendered with scrupulous accuracy—the scratchiness of the characters in the notebook, the dog-eared and wrinkled pages of the reader—yet it is not entirely clear how the notebook and reader are positioned relative to each other, or to the lantern above. A clear representation of these relationships would require that the distance between the painter and each individ-

Takahashi Yuichi, *Reader and Notebook* (*Tokuhon to sōshi*). Kotohiragū Shrine Museum.

ual subject be translated to the canvas in a fixed relationship. Yuichi, however, ignores those distances, approaching the subjects as closely as he can. Individual subjects are represented, but the space they inhabit is not. (Again, this is not meant as a judgment of value. *Reader and Notebook* is one of my favorite paintings.)

In other works by Yuichi in the museum's collection, including *Miniature Pagoda and Armored Sleeve* (*Hyakumantō to gaishū zu*), *Tofu* (*Tōfu*), and *Cod and Plum Blossoms* (*Tara baika*), a certain depth is created by drawing from a slightly raised perspective, looking down on the subjects, and placing chopping boards or stands at an angle to the plane of the picture. These methods, however, are traditional conventions of Japanese art. Inspired by Western painting, Yuichi's eye was faithful to the truth of individual subjects, but when translating those subjects to the canvas, he deployed not a Western but a Japanese form of seeing. In Yuichi's case, of course, this was probably unconscious—which no doubt made it all the more firmly rooted. And when Yuichi's faithful eye was most in accord with this Japanese form of seeing that sought to ignore distance and flatten the entire picture, the result was masterpieces like *Salmon* (*Sake*) and *Grand Courtesan* (*Oiran*) (both in the collection of the Tokyo University of the Arts).

As it happens, *Grand Courtesan* is another portrait of a subject captured at an angle, just like *Philibert Rivière* and *Chin-Jung* (albeit without an armchair). What is more, while Yuichi's subject has her face turned firmly away

Takahashi Yuichi, *Salmon (Sake)*.
The University Art Museum, Tokyo
University of the Arts. Photo: The
University Art Museum, Tokyo
University of the Arts / DNPartcom

Takahashi Yuichi, *Grand Courtesan (Oiran)*. The
University Art Museum, Tokyo University of the
Arts. Photo: The University Art Museum, Tokyo
University of the Arts / DNPartcom

from the viewer, her upper body is a flat, depthless mass, again like Chin-Jung. Perhaps it would be more accurate to say that the commanding form of seeing in *Grand Courtesan* reappears in *Chin-Jung* over half a century later.

There is a gulf between *Grand Courtesan* and *Chin-Jung*, of course, comparable to the one that separates Ingres and Cézanne. Above all, Yasui learned Western art over an extended sojourn in the West, mastering its techniques before returning to Japan. Even so, when I recognize in *Portrait of Chin-Jung* a form of seeing that has more in common with Yuichi than Cézanne, I cannot help but feel moved. Yasui faced a singular challenge: to engage the West without losing himself to it entirely. In a way, we face the same challenge today.

4. The "Trailing Bough" Motif

— 1 —

Unlike the prolific correspondent Van Gogh, or Cézanne with his predilection for logical analysis, Monet wrote relatively little about his own work. One text we do have is his rebuttal to criticism of an exhibition of his *Water Lilies* paintings held in May 1909 at the Galerie Durand-Ruel. In the essay, published in the *Gazette des beaux-arts*, Monet first insists that his *Water Lilies* series is the result of faithful observation of nature, and then adds the following noteworthy lines:

> If you absolutely must . . . find an affiliation for me, put me with the Japanese of old: the refinement of their taste has always appealed to me, and I approve of the suggestions of their aesthetic, which evokes presence by shadow, the whole by the fragment.[1]

Monet also claims "affiliation" with "the European painters of the eighteenth century," but his admiration of "the Japanese of old" is beyond doubt. Monet owned nearly three hundred ukiyo-e prints, most of which were displayed on the walls at his home in Giverny.[2]

This comment from Monet is well known today as a key moment in *japonisme*, but it is worth noting that he recognizes an "aesthetic" of evoking "the presence by the shadow, the whole by the fragment." For a time in his youth, Monet was drawn to exotic elements like kimonos and fans, but evidently at this point he was more concerned with the aesthetics of pictorial composition—that is, with how a painting should be.

Evoking "the presence by the shadow" refers to techniques that seek to bring the presence of something outside the picture into the work, such as painting reflections of clouds and trees on a lake. By using these techniques, a painter can show the wider world around them, rather than only the visible part before their eyes. They might even depict things directly behind them. In that sense, the picture becomes fundamentally the same as a mirror: presences are known by the images they cast rather than directly.

Indeed, after quoting the same essay in his book *Monet: Water Lilies*, Charles Stuckey offers, as a predecessor to Monet's painting of images on water, Manet's *A Bar at the Folies-Bergère*.[3] However, the tradition in Western art of using mirrors to add complexity to a depicted space dates back much further. Jan van Eyck's *Arnolfini Portrait* and Diego Velázquez's *The Ladies-in-Waiting* are magnificent examples of how painters from the Renaissance on have used mirrors to expand, diversify, and add dimensions to pictorial space.[4] Monet's originality lies in the way he allows the water's surface to fill the canvas, turning the entire picture into a mirror instead of introducing a smaller mirror within it. Japanese art was undoubtedly an influence, but in representing "the presence by the shadow," Monet was within the Western tradition.

Representing "the whole by the fragment," on the other hand, is a technique clearly originating in *japonisme*. As one of the most extreme and important examples, consider the "trailing bough" motif, in which a tree branch, or even just a few leaves, enters the frame from above. The canvas known as "Morning with Willows" from the huge *Water Lilies* set at the Musée de l'Orangerie in Paris is an excellent case in point. The surface of the pond fills the entire canvas, but against this background, Monet depicts the near-vertical trunks of the willows on the shore, rising into the frame from below and disappearing out of frame above. To the left and right of each trunk, willow boughs droop into the frame from above.

Unlike the use of mirrors, the trailing bough motif was not used in Western art before Monet's time. Rather, it was discovered by the West in Japanese art, as was the related technique of showing only part of a vast tree's trunk, cut off by the edges of the frame—another example of evoking "the whole by the fragment."

Claude Monet, "Morning with Willows" (Le Matin aux saules), *Water Lilies* (*Nymphéas*). Musée de l'Orangerie in Paris. Photo © RMN-Grand Palais (musée de l'Orangerie) / Michel Urtado / Distributed by AMF-DNPartcom

One of Monet's main inspirations was surely Hiroshige's "Inside Kameido Tenjin Shrine" (*Kameido Tenjin keidai*) from *One Hundred Famous Views of Edo* (*Meisho Edo hyakkei*). In this print, a twisted wisteria branch is partly visible on the left, but not visibly connected to the large clump of wisteria blossoms that descends into the frame from above. The print was not in Monet's collection,[5] but given Hiroshige's popularity in France at the end of the nineteenth century and Monet's comments after the Galerie Durand-Ruel exhibition, it is difficult to imagine that Monet did not know it. We might also note *The Water-Lily Pond*, painted in 1899, which has essentially the same composition as Hiroshige's print, including the arched bridge at the center.[6] However, in this painting, along with many others with similar compositions, Monet's interest is clearly directed at the central bridge and the pond of water lilies below. The trailing bough motif appears only in the partial background depiction of a willow on the left, whereas in Hiroshige's work it is far more important. Trailing boughs would not truly assert their presence in Monet's work until the much later large-scale paintings now held at the Musée de l'Orangerie. Presumably, this means the motif took some getting used to, even for Monet. We can also attribute its glorious proliferation in later works to the fact that his conception of the *Water Lilies* series itself had developed as well.

— 2 —

Absent from traditional Western art, the trailing bough motif was widely used in Japan, particularly in the early modern period. Trailing boughs appear not just in prints and paintings but also as design elements in other kinds of arts and crafts. From the start, the Japanese displayed a strong affection for the "broken branch paintings" imported from China, and in the Momoyama period, a decorative technique arose of showing trees in close-up extending up and out of the frame with branches descending back into it. This idea developed along diverse lines throughout the Edo period. The most skillful and impressive uses of the motif is found in works like Ogata Kōrin's *Red and White Plum Blossoms* (*Kōhakubai-zu byōbu*) (p. 85) and Maruyama Ōkyo's *Wisteria* (*Fujihana-zu byōbu*). Trees and plants that naturally lend themselves to this treatment—weeping willows, wisteria, trailing vines—were used in everything from large-scale compositions to craft designs, as is clear from works like *Narrow Path with Ivy* (*Tsuta no hosomichi byōbu*), attributed to Tawaraya Sōtatsu's studio, and the many poem scrolls and other collaborations between

Top: Claude Monet, *The Water-Lily Pond* (*Nymphéas*). The National Gallery, London. Photo © The National Gallery, London / Distributed by AMF-DNPatcom
Bottom: Utagawa Hiroshige, "Inside Kameido Tenjin Shrine" (*Kameido Tenjin keidai*), *One Hundred Famous Views of Edo* (*Meisho Edo hyakkei*). Edo-Tokyo Museum. Photo: Tokyo Metropolitan Foundation for History and Culture Image Archive

Sōtatsu's school and calligrapher Hon'ami Kōetsu.

The trailing bough was also a common feature of the ukiyo-e so beloved

Maruyama Ōkyo, *Wisteria Screen (Fujihana-zu byōbu)* (right screen). Nezu Museum.

by the nineteenth-century West. Hiroshige's *One Hundred Famous Views of Edo* includes not only the aforementioned "Inside Kameido Tenjin Shrine" but also works like "Yatsumi Bridge" (*Yatsumi no hashi*) and "Ayase River and Kanegafuchi" (*Ayasegawa kanegafuchi*) that use this motif to add a close-up effect to the foreground. In works like Suzuki Harunobu's *Shirabyōshi Dancer in a Boat* (*Asazumabune*), the motif is all but pure symbol. In the Edo period, the trailing bough was so well known that it verged on cliché. Nevertheless, Western artists did not think to use it until they came into contact with Japanese art. This in itself is highly intriguing, and the reasons for it go beyond a single motif to encompass the nature of visual art and how it is viewed in different cultures.

As Monet rightly observed, evoking "the whole by the fragment" is one of Japanese art's chief characteristics. The trailing bough is just one particularly representative example of this. As well as flora, Japanese painters were masters of evoking boats, bridges, and even people by showing only the tiniest part of them in the image. Nor was Monet the only one to realize this. Many commentators in the age of *japonisme* pointed out this technique as a major difference between Japanese and Western aesthetics. Ernest Chesneau, in his 1878 essay "Le Japon à Paris," included "unexpectedness of composition" alongside "originality of pictorial effect" and "richness of tone" as traits of Japanese art,[7] and this "unexpectedness" came mostly from free-roaming perspective and bold trimming that cut away most of the subject. The April

Utagawa Hiroshige, "Ayase River and Kanegafuchi" (*Ayasegawa kanegafuchi*), *One Hundred Famous Views of Edo* (*Meisho Edo hyakkei*). Image: National Diet Library Collections

Suzuki Harunobu, *Shirabyōshi Dancer in a Boat* (*Asazumabune*). Collection of Art Research Center, Ritsumeikan University Z0166-407

1891 edition of *Artistic Japan* includes an essay by Roger Marx titled "On the Role and Influence of the Arts of the Far East and of Japan" in which he identifies "isolated or half-finished composition" and "the evocation of a whole by means of a fragment" as important contributions by Japanese artists. Richard Muther, in the revised 1907 edition of *The History of Modern Painting*, credits Japanese artists with having taught their European counterparts "the surprise, the fleeting hint, the way of increasing effect by the incompletion of motive, the suggestion of the whole by a part."[8]

Of course, while the trailing bough is not found in the West, Mannerist and Baroque paintings (for example) do contain examples of human figures cut off by the edge of the frame. However, this only happens when the truncation has a particular meaning, or the figure so treated is more or less unconnected to the main subject. None of these instances of cropping is as extreme as Hiroshige's "Haneda Ferry and Benten Shrine" (*Haneda no watashi, Benten no yashiro*), where the main subject is reduced to a pair of arms and one leg.

Presumably, this is because of the idea current in the West, particularly during and after the Renaissance, that each painting must be a microcosm—a world complete in itself, independent of its surrounding environment and space. Alberti compared paintings to windows, but he did not mean that they should open onto some arbitrary part of the vastness of nature; within each window, a world should be constructed, ordered, and completed. Put another way, in the West, the edges of a painting sever the image from its surroundings, and those edges are regulated with according strictness. Such a worldview could never permit boughs or sprays of flowers drooping in from above to become established as a motif.

Utagawa Hiroshige, "Haneda Ferry and Benten Shrine" (*Haneda no watashi, Benten no yashiro*), *One Hundred Famous Views of Edo* (*Meisho Edo hyakkei*), Museum of Fine Arts, Boston. Image: William Sturgis Bigelow Collection 11.17015
Photo © 2021 Museum of Fine Arts, Boston. All Rights Reserved. c/o DNPartcom

In contrast, the Japanese art world took a much more relaxed attitude to regulating the edges of the pictorial space. Indeed, to allow a visible "fragment" to hint at and evoke an undepicted "whole," painter and viewer needed to share an unspoken understanding that space extended, unchanged in quality, beyond the edges of what was actually depicted. Kōrin's plum tree is cut off by the edge of the picture, but it continues to exist outside it, even reemerging into the frame elsewhere. It is this continuity between the picture's interior and exterior that allowed the trailing bough motif to take root in Japanese art—an "aesthetic of continuity" rather than the "aesthetic of completeness" seen in the West.

This ideal of continuity permeates all aspects of Japanese culture, including architecture, urban design, theater, and even daily life, in addition to art.[9] It also explains why *japonisme* was able to transcend exoticism and offer an entirely new aesthetic to the West, where the "aesthetic of completeness" upheld since the Renaissance was nearing bankruptcy.[10] At any rate, this is how Monet thought of *japonisme* in his final years, and it is surely no coincidence that the *Water Lilies* series of that period, so rich in "trailing boughs," also rejected the pictorial limitations in place since the Renaissance and gradually spread left and right until it came to enfold the painter (and therefore the viewer) in a single vast, circular composition.

— 3 —

Another fascinating fact: the meeting of Japan and the West through the trailing bough motif can be observed not only in French but also in Japanese art history. The quintessential, and therefore most meaningful, example is surely Shiba Kōkan.

Kōkan was one of the "Westernists" who made up the most radical school of painting in eighteenth-century Edo. "A painting that is not realistic cannot be beautiful, and does not deserve to be painted at all," he thundered in *Seiyō gadan* (Discussion of Western art), and firmly believed that only "Western styles" could achieve that realism. He pursued the study of Western art with all his energy and every means at his disposal at the time. This only makes it more surprising when, in one of his oil paintings—and one clearly based on a Western model, at that—we spy an extremely Japanese trailing branch. That painting is *The Cooper* (*Taruzukuri*).

As many critics have observed, the painting is based on "Cooper" (*Kuiper*) from *The Book of Trades* (*Het menselyk bedryf*), a collection of illustrations by the father–son team Jan and Caspar Luyken. *The Book of Trades* was apparently something of a vade mecum for Kōkan, who lifted many other images from it as well. In the case of "Cooper," however, he created not one but two derivative works: a more or less faithful copy in ink,

Shiba Kōkan, *The Cooper* (*Taruzukuri*) (oil painting). Tokyo National Museum. Image: TNM Image Archives.

Jan and Casper Luyken, "Cooper" (*Kuiper*), *The Book of Trades* (*Het menselyk bedryf*).

Shiba Kōkan, *The Cooper* (*Taruzukuri*) (ink drawing).

and an oil painting that expands the original square composition to a wider landscape aspect. The drawing is more or less the same as the original, but Kōkan introduces several modifications to the painting. While the cooper himself is much like the Luykens' version, his position in the frame and the buildings behind him are not. The largest change is the inclusion of a tree leaning in from the left and rising out of the frame—and a trailing bough

Takahashi Yuichi, *Shinobazu Pond* (*Shinobazu no ike*). Aichi Prefectural Museum of Art.

reentering the frame from above. The original, of course, includes nothing like this.

The addition of this distinctive motif thoroughly "Japanizes" the image, but I doubt Kōkan did that intentionally, or even consciously. After all, he believed that Chinese and Japanese art was "child's play" compared to the art of the West. It seems more likely that the trailing bough motif had simply penetrated Kōkan's artistic sensibilities so deeply that it took up permanent residence there. Tradition can be a stubborn thing.

The same tendency appears in the work of Kōkan's self-appointed spiritual successor Takahashi Yuichi. Of Yuichi's passion there is no need to speak; he devoted his life to the mastery of Western painting. Nevertheless, there in his *Shinobazu Pond* (*Shinobazu no ike*) are boughs drooping into the foreground from above, swaying in the wind. As with Kōkan, the motif was likely hidden so deeply in his sensibilities that he did not realize the implications of deploying it.

Fujishima Takeji, another Western-style painter, did not reject the art of

Fujishima Takeji, *Tivoli, Pond at Villa d'Este*
(*Tivori, Vira Deste no ike*). The University Art
Museum, Tokyo University of the Arts.
Photo: The University Art Museum, Tokyo
University of the Arts / DNPartcom

Wada Eisaku, *Entertainment in the Fields*
(*Noasobi*). The University Art Museum,
Tokyo University of the Arts.
Photo: The University Art Museum,
Tokyo University of the Arts / DNPartcom

Japan as firmly as Kōkan and Yuichi. Even so, when we notice the prominent trailing boughs in *Tivoli, Pond at Villa d'Este* (*Tivori, Vira Deste no ike*), which he painted during his time in Italy, they feel less a calculated move than a spontaneous revelation of his own sensibilities.

Together, these works illustrate the sheer persistence of the trailing bough motif—and the Japanese sensibilities that birthed and cultivated it.[11] Furthermore, the appearance of the motif in early Japanese oil painting shows that, despite a certain degree of copying and recopying of European models, the history of oil painting in Japan can securely be located within the history of Japanese sensibilities more broadly.

We might also sense a connection to the fact that so many Western-style Japanese painters of the Meiji and later periods returned to Japanese painting styles in their final years. Consider *Entertainment in the Fields* (*Noasobi*) by Wada Eisaku, who followed Kuroda Seiki and Okada Saburōsuke in studying under Raphaël Collin in France. This oil painting was shown at the sixth Teiten Exhibition in 1925. Its clear and intricate draftsmanship, pure and multihued coloring, and decorative composition set it apart from works like *Kodama*, painted in France a quarter of a century earlier, and indeed make it reminiscent of a traditional Japanese painting. And there, falling into frame above the female figures in ancient-looking dress with a vaguely (if rather oversweet) Historical Romanticist air, are sprays of wisteria.

Notes

1. Roger Marx, "Les Nymphéas de M. Claude Monet," *Gazette des beaux-arts* (June 1909), 528.
2. For Monet's ukiyo-e collection, see Kobayashi Toshinobu, "Kurōdo Mone ukiyoe hanga korekushon," *Japonezurī kenkyū gakkaihō* 3 (1948), 11–29. The article contains a list based on Kobayashi's survey of works in Monet's collection. Note that part of this collection was displayed in Japan. See the catalog for *Mone to ukiyoe* exhibition at Tokyo Nihonbashi Mitsukoshi in October 1983.
3. Charles F. Stuckey, *Monet: Water Lilies* (New York: Hugh Lauter Levin, 1988), 18. (Japanese edition translated by Takashina Shūji and Matsumoto Erika and published by Chūō Kōronsha in 1988.)
4. See André Chastel's classic article, "Le tableau dans le tableau" (1964), in his *Fables, formes, figures* (Paris: Flammarion, 1978); Heinrich Schwarz's "The Mirror in Art," *Art Quarterly* 15, no. 2 (Summer 1952), 96–118; and Jurgis Baltrušaitis's *Le Miroir* (Paris: Elmayan, 1978).
5. Kobayashi, "Kurōdo Mone."
6. The relationship between these two has been noted by many authors, including Yamada Chisaburō in *Ukiyoe to inshōha* (*Kindai no bijutsu*, Vol. 18) (Tokyo: Shibundō, 1973), 64–67.
7. Ernest Chesneau, "Le Japon à Paris," *Gazette des beaux-arts* (September 1878), 387.
8. All these quotations are included in the catalog for the *Le Japonisme* exhibition held in 1988 at the National Museum of Western Art, Tokyo, and the Grand Palais, Paris.
9. *Nihon no bigaku* 2: *Tokushū, "Renzoku"* (July 1984).
10. This new aesthetic is deeply connected to the arrival of the camera, which allowed for the impartial extraction of sections of space as photographs, but I will save that discussion for another occasion.
11. The trailing bough motif is frequently seen in *nihonga*, modern artworks that uphold traditional Japanese painting techniques and conventions. Examples include Yokoyama Taikan's *Floating Lanterns* (*Ryūtō*, 1909) and Hishida Shunsō's *Black Cat* (*Kuroki Neko*, 1910).

5. The Art of the Journey

— 1 —

The third and final volume of the *Shigisan engi* (Legends of Mount Shigi) picture-scroll follows a Buddhist nun as she travels to Nara in search of her brother, the monk Myōren. The scroll begins with the heroine's departure from the mountains of Shinano province (modern-day Nagano), which the opening text describes as follows:

> At this time, Myōren had an older sister in Shinano. Not having seen him in some years, she thought, "Alas, I have not seen that young monk since he went to Tōdaiji temple to confirm his vows. What has happened to him? I am concerned, so I shall visit him," and left for Nara. When she visited the passage between Yamashinadera and Tōdaiji . . . [1]

The text leaps straight from the nun's decision to go to Nara to her arrival there, without any explanation of the long journey in between. However, the scroll's illustrations tell a different story. Starting with an image of the nun on horseback following a valley road between towering mountains, they show a host of detailed scenes from her travels: asking directions from a villager beneath a willow tree, resting inside a home at the owner's invitation, and walking with a staff on a mountain trail beside frolicking deer. The images include elements of genre painting that convey a sense of daily life at the time: people doing laundry, sewing, planting vegetables beneath a blossoming peach tree—even dogs playing in the road. As viewers, we follow the picture-scroll's progress as it traces the journey of the nun and her retinue, crossing mountains, traversing valleys, and passing through villages.

The scenes between the nun's departure from Shinano and her arrival at Tōdaiji in Nara take up a sizeable portion of the scroll's length: over six meters out of a total fourteen. Given that just over two of those fourteen meters are text, this means roughly half of the scroll's pictorial space is devoted to a journey described with a half-sentence of text. On one hand, this is a skillful technique allowing viewers to experience the long journey from Shinano to Nara themselves; on the other, it reflects the Japanese people's fondness for artistic representations of travel.

In a paper entitled "The Wilderness Journey," Penelope Mason of Florida State University argues that there is a philosophical reason why Japanese picture- scrolls so often depict the hero traveling through nature. In this nun's journey, she discerns a Buddhist message—specifically, the esoteric Shingon Buddhism thought of Kūkai. According to Mason, because Kūkai taught that every tree and blade of grass had Buddha-nature, contact with nature was thought to hold the potential for enlightenment, and the nun embarks on just such a "voyage to enlightenment." The artist's emphasis on the travels of the nun highlights nature's dual power to enlighten and purify, and the picture-scroll itself has a dual structure showing two paths: Myōren develops mysterious powers through harsh training, while his sister attains enlightenment by roaming through nature.[2]

This would make the nun's extended pictorial travelogue suitably edifying for a picture-scroll of the *engi* genre, which typically explains the history of a temple with reference to legends and miracles involving its founder. Given that the idea of Buddha-nature in every blade of grass is indeed found in Japanese Buddhism, along with the strong cultural predilection for nature worship, it is quite plausible that depictions of nature in Japanese art differ from landscape painting in the West. However, interpreting the nun's journey as a theological representation of finding enlightenment in nature seems to me a rather strained hypothesis. Aside from the fact that the written text does not even hint at this, the pictures themselves reject such an analysis.

Yes, the scroll shows the nun deep in the mountains, surrounded by deer. But just as important—if not more so—are the images of her asking for di-

Detail of vol.3 of *Legends of Mount Shigi* (*Shigisan engi*) picture-scroll. Chōgosonshiji temple. Image: National Diet Library Collections

rections and enjoying spirited conversation with the people she meets along the way, as well as the depictions of their daily lives. The nun's image appears a total of five times in her journey, but only two of these appearances show her "traveling through nature." In the other three appearances, she is interacting with villagers. It seems that the artist intentionally depicted contact not only with nature but also with what we might call the "lay world" of human emotion and custom. From treacherous mountain roads to remote, unknown villages, the nun experienced nothing that any other traveler of the time would not have encountered as well.

— 2 —

But, in that case, why does travel make up such a large part of the *Shigisan engi*? And not just this work—as Mason observes, Japanese art abounds with depictions of travel. Mason offers picture-scrolls like *Saigyō monogatari* (Tales of Saigyō) and Iwasa Matabē's *Oguri Hangan* as further examples of her thesis of natural enlightenment, and, whether one agrees with this thesis or not, travel scenes undoubtably play an enormous role in these works. Countless other examples could be cited, like the picture-scroll biography of Ippen, which consists almost entirely of travel scenes, or Hiroshige's *Fifty-Three Stations of the Tōkaidō*. Can simple love of travel explain this? Nor is the phenomenon limited to pictorial art: travel writing was a far more important genre in Japan than in the West. The two cultures, it seems, thought about travel in very different ways.

Images of travel were not, of course, entirely absent from Western art. Restricting the discussion to Christian themes, to correspond to the Buddhist narratives (*setsuwa*) of Japan, the first example that comes to mind is the Flight into Egypt. This comes from the passage in the Bible where Joseph, Mary, and the infant Jesus flee to Egypt to escape King Herod's Massacre of the Innocents. As a key episode in the life of both Mary and Jesus, it was popular among medieval and later painters. Most paintings on this theme show the entire holy family on their travels: Mary, holding Jesus in her arms, riding a donkey led by Joseph. In the Renaissance, artists became fond of a new theme known as "Rest on the Flight into Egypt." In these works, Mary and Jesus are depicted at rest in sprawling landscapes. Paintings by Joachim Patinir and Claude Lorrain in the sixteenth and seventeenth centuries respectively are almost entirely landscape, with Mary and Jesus appearing only as tiny figures in the foreground or middle ground. "Pure" landscape painting emerged as a genre much later in the West than in Japan, and the role of the Flight into Egypt in that process cannot be overlooked.

However, despite the superficial thematic similarity, paintings of the Flight into Egypt are very different from the nun's journey in *Shigisan engi*. Consider Giotto di Bondone's well-known mural on the wall of the Scrovegni Chapel in Padua. Mary and the infant Jesus sit on their donkey at the very center of the image, with stony mountains in the background and Joseph and others to their left and right. The focus of the work is the holy mother and child. The landscape is mere background, and the other figures are peripheral. It may be a painting of "travelers," but not of "travel" as such. Certainly it is not the kind of temporally and spatially developed depiction of travel seen in *Shigisan engi*, which depicts the traveler winding through valleys, hiking steep mountain trails, and meeting villagers and seeing how they live. The edges of Giotto's painting frame a world complete in itself and therefore fixed.

In fact, most paintings of the Flight into Egypt share this characteristic. Even works like Patinir's and Lorrain's, which emphasize the landscape rather than the holy family, are the same on that point. Claude's *Rest on the Flight into Egypt*, like most of his paintings, essentially uses the Biblical theme as an excuse to draw the landscape—but that excuse did not have to involve travel. These are free-standing landscapes, complete in themselves, not scenes appearing one after another before a traveler's eyes. Landscapes are a highly important element in travel art, of course, but not every depiction of nature is a travel scene, any more than the depiction of nature that opens Sei Shonagon's *Pillow Book*—"In spring, the dawn; the mountains brighten at the edges, growing paler . . ."—is travel writing.

Swiss-born Herbert Plutschow's *Tabi suru Nihonjin* (The traveling Japanese), an intriguing exploration of medieval Japanese travel literature, ends with a chapter comparing Japanese and European travel with travel literature and diaries in the medieval period.[3] Plutschow notes that, in contrast to the profusion of travel literature in Japan, this genre was virtually non existent in Europe until the Renaissance. What's more, even the Renaissance examples are rare; true travel writing does not appear in Europe until the Romantic era of the late eighteenth century. Plutschow attributes this to different views of and attitudes toward nature. The Japanese favor "dialogue" with nature, feel close to it, and under the influence of Buddhism even choose nature as a place to attain enlightenment. Europeans, however, averted their eyes from natural beauty, seeing praise of nature as blasphemy against God.

Note the correspondence to Mason's interpretation of the nun's journey in *Shigisan engi*. Plutschow's views on Japanese travel art from a Western perspective are, like Mason's, highly intriguing—but this is perhaps why they also feel somehow unsatisfying. The issue seems to be this: in taking "views of nature" as a starting point, both authors associate travel with praise of nature and discovery of natural beauty. As a result, their comparisons of Japanese and Western travel writing are unbalanced in both directions: Japanese works are considered solely in terms of interactions with the natural world (for example, Mason focuses almost entirely on the nun's journey through nature, overlooking her contact with villagers), while any Western work that praises nature is considered fit for comparison, whether it is truly about travel or not.

Interaction with nature was an undeniably important part of Japanese depictions of travel, but at the same time we cannot ignore the human element in these works: descriptions of local customs, habits, sentiments, and history. Even Bashō, the "poet of nature" who set out for the Deep North "like a scrap of cloud before the wind, with a ceaseless desire to roam," remains in constant dialogue with those who came before him, and takes an interest in everything from the name of the girl running behind his horse to the fact that he slept under the same roof as some prostitutes. The fascination among literati with the human world amid the natural one would ultimately flower into picaresque novels like Jippensha Ikku's *Shank's Mare* (*Tōkaidōchū Hizakurige*). On the other hand, just as traveling to the Alps and painting a splendid landscape there does not a "travel painting" make, Petrarch and Sannazaro's hymns to the natural world, however exquisite, are not travel writing.

— 3 —

Discrepancies like this most likely result from different conceptions of travel itself. In Japan, travel unfolded continuously in time and space, accompanied by a broad range of interactions with the human and natural worlds in an environment that differed from everyday life. Artwork about travel depicted these interactions in a continuous manner, sometimes through color and form and sometimes through words. This description is as applicable to the nun's journey in *Shigisan engi* as it is to Bashō's *Narrow Road to the Deep*

North (*Oku no hosomichi*) or Ikku's *Shank's Mare*. In the West, however, travel meant going to a place outside of everyday life. It was the experience at that destination that mattered, not the process of getting there. To choose an example that falls neatly between *Narrow Road* and *Shank's Mare* in chronological terms, *Gulliver's Travels* may be a fantasy, but Jonathan Swift's focus remains firmly on the events in Brobdingnag and Lilliput rather than the journey to these places.

In other words, travel in the West was about the destination, while in Japan it was about the journey. Consider the pilgrimages that Plutschow uses as an example. The custom of traveling to a distant site for religious reasons is found in both Japan and the West. In Europe, however, the destinations were clearly defined at an early stage, and the aim of a pilgrimage was to arrive at one of them, whether that meant Jerusalem, the Cathedral of Santiago de Compostela in Spain, or a less popular destination like Rome or Lourdes. Of course pilgrims visited many churches as they went, but those churches were simply waystations; the pilgrimage followed a straight line directly to its terminus.

In Japan, however, the word for pilgrimage includes the character 巡, meaning "to go around, to circulate." The journey was a circle, not a straight line. According to scholar of Buddhist folklore Gorai Shigeru, "going around" a tree, temple, rock, or mountain was a common religious practice since ancient times, and these smaller circuits eventually evolved into medieval pilgrimage trails with thirty-three or more temples.[4] The custom of *hyakudo mairi*, walking a set route on the grounds of a shrine a hundred times, might also be considered a remnant of these ancient ways. Note, too, that if one is "going around," the destination is also the starting point, so reaching it cannot be the goal. The actual process of "going around" is the objective—not arriving at a single final temple, but visiting each temple along the way. In this respect, works like *Narrow Road to the Deep North* also depict journeys of pilgrimage.

To return to the subject of painting, if the goal is to depict the process of the journey rather than its final destination—that is, the variety of experience as it unfolds continuously in space and time—the Japanese picture-scroll is clearly an ideal format. On the other hand, the Western painting with its self-contained world in a fixed frame is more suited to depicting a destination or a single stop along the way: an isolated scene rather than a continuous world. (Works like the *Fifty-Three Stations of the Tōkaidō* combine many isolated prints into a continuous series.) Naturally, this correspondence between form and content is not a simple matter of cause and effect. Both form and content seem to arise from something deeper—a shared way of thinking, even a worldview—but the aesthetic issues this raises are worthy of an essay of their own.

Notes

1. Chino Kaori, *Shigisan engi emaki* (*Meihō Nihon no bijutsu* 11) (Tokyo: Shōgakukan, 1982), 73.
2. Penelope E. Mason, "The Wilderness Journey: The Soteric Value of Nature in Japanese Narrative Painting," in *Art the Ape of Nature: Studies in Honor of H. W. Janson*, ed. Moshe Barasch, Lucy Freeman Sandler, and Patricia Egan (New York: H. N. Abrams, 1981), 67–90.
3. Herbert E. Plutschow, *Tabi suru Nihonjin: Nihon no chūsei kikō bungaku o saguru* (Tokyo: Musashino Shoin), 1983.
4. Gorai Shigeru, "Yugyō to junrei," in Gorai Shigeru, *Nihon no tabibito* (*Asahi karuchā bukkusu* 21) (Osaka: Ōsaka shoseki), 1983.

6. The Principle of Ornamentation

Characterizing Japanese Art

The *japonisme* of late nineteenth-century Europe was driven by more than mere exoticism. The artists of Europe were also inspired by the fresh and surprising forms of creative expression they saw in woodblock prints, standing screens, and other items imported from Japan. Japanese art had a range of characteristics not previously seen in Western art, and these captured the imagination of Europe's artistic community.

French critic Ernest Chesneau was one of the first to take interest in Japanese art. In his 1869 lecture "L'art japonais," he listed three unique characteristics of Japanese art as seen on screens, illustrations in books, and handcrafts: asymmetry, stylization, and use of color. Later, in an extended critical essay for the 1878 Exposition Universelle entitled "Le Japon à Paris," he expanded on this, explaining that what connoisseurs admired in Japanese art was "the unexpectedness of its compositions, the science of its forms, the richness of its colors, the originality of its pictorial effects, and . . . the simplicity of the means employed to obtain these results." Note that Chesneau focuses not on superficial motifs like kimonos and fans but on purely creative characteristics such as composition and color. If contemporary European artists welcomed these characteristics as guideposts toward new expressive possibilities, we can only conclude that they were not found in Western painting beforehand.

Indeed, until the arrival of Manet and the Impressionists in the late nineteenth century, Western painting was still oriented around methods for re-creating reality that were established in the Renaissance. Specifically, this meant depicting three-dimensional spaces and subjects as they appeared to the eye, using techniques like perspective, shading, and modeling. Although each period, region, and school had its own approach, these variations all

Views In and Around Kyoto (Rakuchū rakugai-zu)—Ikeda version (detail).
Hayashibara Museum of Art. Photo: Hayashibara Museum of Art / DNPartcom

existed within shared boundaries. Realism, in the sense of "re-creating reality," remained the unshaken foundation of Western painting from Renaissance Classicism to nineteenth-century Academism.

Japanese art did not seek to depict a three-dimensional world in this way. On the contrary, it respected and even emphasized the fundamental two-dimensionality of its medium. This does not mean, of course, that Japanese artists ignored the unfolding of space or the relative locations of human and other subjects within it. Spatial relationships are clearly depicted in land-scapes, narrative paintings (*monogatari-e*), and other genres where they are important. The "in and around the capital" paintings of the early modern period show the intricate spatial construction of the city's sprawl, including the location of specific buildings, and even its residents, with perfect clarity. The difference between Japan and the West lies not in whether these things are depicted, but how.

As we saw in the first chapter of this book, Western perspective and shad-ing fixes the painter's perspective at a single point, like the lens of a camera. Distant subjects are small and faint, while nearer subjects are large and vivid. In "in and around the capital" paintings, however, the perspective roams freely through and even above the town. Buildings are shown from above to better convey the town's structure, while each figure and street scene is depicted as if the painter were right beside them. This makes the painting an aggregation of partial scenes viewed from differing perspectives.

Similar techniques are used for interior scenes in works like the *Genji Monogatari* picture-scroll. Human figures are shown from a horizontal perspective, while buildings are depicted from above to clarify their internal construction and floor plans. Roofs and interior walls and screens would block the view, so they are omitted to create what are called "roofless house" (*fukinuki-yatai*) depictions. Here we see another characteristic of Japanese art: a principle of simplification in which whatever is not necessary is cut away.

The Art of Elimination

To summarize, while Western painting (at least from the Renaissance on) involves depicting the world from a single, fixed perspective, Japanese painting entails the arrangement of elements viewed from different perspectives. These perspectives, however, are not chosen arbitrarily; each is the most appropriate to represent its particular subject. Urban spaces are clearest when viewed from above, while the outlines of the human form are most recognizable when viewed from the side. The accumulation of these elements makes the image expand outward. This is why Western painting emphasizes depth perpendicular to the canvas but Japanese painting emphasizes flatness parallel to it.

These contrasting approaches to expression reflect differences in fundamental attitudes toward painting and indeed patterns of thought in general. In the West, the painter's perspective is absolute, and the painted subjects must be made to obey it. In Japan, the painted subjects take precedence; the painter must adopt the appropriate perspective for each so that they can exist side-by-side. We might see this as indicative of the difference between the unified worldview of the West, where a single center has absolute value, and the pluralism of Japan, where multiple values can coexist.

In any case, if the Western approach reflects a "principle of realism," in the sense that the goal is to create the illusion of the three-dimensional world before the painter's eyes, Japanese painting must reflect a "principle of ornamentation" in which the two-dimensional surface is filled with flattened partial images, each depicting a single subject with proper esteem for that subject's characteristics. The rich colors, unexpected compositions, and other characteristics of Japanese art praised by Chesneau all derive from this principle. Its absence from Western tradition suggests that it is extremely Japanese in nature, and therefore had an enormous impact on Western painters when they discovered it—just as the Western principle of realism, hitherto unknown in Japan, was a fresh, startling idea to Japanese painters like Shiba Kōkan and Takahashi Yuichi.

Japonisme was not the first instance of Japanese aesthetics finding an audience outside Japan. Even in the West, handcrafts like lacquerware and ceramics were known as early as the sixteenth century. But the earliest non-Japanese commentary on Japanese art, dating to the medieval period, was written not in the West but instead much closer to the source: China. The *Xuanhe huapu* (Xuanhe manual of painting) was a collection of over 6,390 paintings with commentary assembled on the orders of Emperor Huizong of the Song dynasty (r. 1100–1125). The preface, dated 1120, describes Japanese art in these terms:

> The names of those who painted the Japanese works in this collection are unknown, but their paintings depict that country's customs, landscapes, and scenery. Their use of color is extremely heavy, with great quantities of gold and blue. They do not necessarily contain truth, seeking only through brilliance and splendor to be seen as beautiful.

Note the mention of strong color deployed for decorative effect. "Gold and blue" here is shorthand for the liberal use of gold and silver dust mixed into paste ("gold") and ultramarine, verdigris, and other mineral paints ("blue"). Art historian Tsuji Nobuo observes in *Nihon bijutsu no hyōjō* (Expressionism in Japanese art) that, in China, it was considered most important to paint what was true, using pure, clean colors. The lavish use of color in Japanese paintings was interpreted as the pursuit of superficial beauty. This is further evidence that Japan had principles of ornamentation all its own.

Although these principles can be viewed as continuous with a tradition that stretches back to prehistoric Jōmon pottery and decorated burial mounds, its most sumptuous and refined expression is found in the so-called "gold-and-blue screen paintings" (*kinpeki shōhekiga*) of the Momoyama period. These paintings adorned the folding screens and sliding room partitions used to divide interior spaces, and their sheer size only heightened their splendor. In Azuchi Castle, built by Oda Nobunaga over three years beginning in 1576, the partitions on every floor bore stunning paintings of flowers, birds, animals, and landscapes by Kanō Eitoku and his students. Although these works were lost along with the castle itself, contemporary records ("every single painting in the reception rooms was golden") survive as testament to their startling beauty. Eitoku's genius may have perfected this form, but painters of the Hasegawa school and many others produced works in the same vein. The result was arguably one of the richest and most magnificent flowerings of Japanese aesthetic sensibilities in history.

Gold was used for its dazzling ornamental effect, but also in two other ways that have a deep formal connection to Japanese aesthetic sensibilities. The first was the use of "fields of gold" to blot out the background. This served to close off a painting's depth and emphasize its flatness instead. The second was the judicious placement of "golden clouds" or "spears of fog" to conceal unnecessary elements in the composition and help the main subjects stand out. This was often seen in "in and around the capital" pictures, where golden clouds fill the spaces between individual street scenes.

One of the most exquisite and refined uses of gold in Japanese painting is Ogata Kōrin's *Irises* (*Kakitsubata-zu byōbu*). This monumental work consists of two six-panel screens adorned with flowering irises on a field of

Ogata Kōrin, *Irises* (*Kakitsubata-zu byōbu*) (right screen). Nezu Museum.

gold—and nothing else. The accompanying elements that a Western painting would have to include to satisfy the principle of realism—the surface of
the water, the edges of the pond, even the sky—are completely omitted. By
covering up everything but his main subject with shimmering gold, Kōrin
created a work that is both extremely simple and startlingly voluptuous.

The story of Sen no Rikyū's single morning glory, briefly covered in
Chapter 1, is similar. Word reached Toyotomi Hideyoshi, by then the ruler
of Japan, that Rikyū was cultivating a rare kind of morning glory in his garden. Learning that Hideyoshi wished to see the blooms, Rikyū invited him to
come and do so. But on the morning of Hideyoshi's visit, Rikyū had every
single morning glory plucked from the garden. When Hideyoshi arrived, he
was deeply displeased, but he allowed Rikyū to usher him into the tea-
room—where the last of the morning glories was on display in the tokonoma
alcove. His mood improved at once.

Both of these examples show how the Japanese sense of beauty prizes
ornamentation but often employs it to eliminate other elements rather than
to fill every free space with decorative detail.

This aesthetic of elimination and negation is also present in the *Western
Kings on Horseback* (*Taisei ōkō kiba zu*) paintings mentioned in Chapter 1—
another Momoyama-period work. So deeply rooted in the Japanese sensibility is the aesthetic that the artist did not hesitate to eliminate what he deemed

Hasegawa Tōhaku, *Pine Trees* (*Shōrin-zu byōbu*). Tokyo National Museum. Image: TNM Image Archives

unnecessary even when directly copying a Western model.

These tendencies are even more apparent in the ink wash paintings that reached their zenith between the Muromachi and Momoyama periods. This medium naturally supports a strict spirit of elimination, with all color except that of the ink rejected, but Japanese artists went further. By boldly leaving vast swathes of white space untouched, they attained a supreme profundity.

Pine Trees (*Shōrin-zu*) is one example. Painted by Hasegawa Tōhaku, a contemporary of Eitoku, the work depicts a grove of pines in the damp morning haze with deep sentiment and a masterful sense of space. Despite the Chinese roots of ink wash painting, these characteristics are overwhelmingly Japanese in nature. We might also note that Tōhaku's use of white space serves the same function as the gleaming fields of gold in works like Kōrin's *Irises*: eliminating the unnecessary to heighten the expressive effect. Richly colored gold-and-blue screen paintings might at first seem the polar opposite of subdued ink wash paintings, but both deploy highly Japanese expressive forms animated by a distinctly Japanese aesthetic.

Attributed to Kanō Eitoku, *Cypress Trees* (*Hinoki-zu byōbu*). Tokyo National Museum.
Source: ColBase (https://colbase.nich.go.jp/)

Close-Up Technique

The expressive technique perfected by Eitoku in his gold-and-blue screen paintings also featured innovative composition. One particularly striking example is his method of depicting subjects only partially and in close-up. In works like *Cypress Trees* (*Hinoki-zu byōbu*), attributed to Eitoku (though not without dissenters), or the paintings by Hasegawa Tōhaku on Chishakuin temple's sliding room partitions, we see massive tree trunks cut off by the top edge of the screen. Sometimes a branch or some leaves will trail back into frame at another point. This technique not only hints at a spatial continuity extending beyond the bounds of the picture, it is also a bold, unusual compositional choice incompatible with the unity of composition required by Western realism.

Unique to Japan, this "aesthetic of the close-up" has no interest in grasping the subject as a whole, denies the painting completeness, and is blithely unconcerned with bilateral stability. As Chesneau observed, it strongly influenced French painters during the period of *japonisme*, inspiring eccen-

Ogata Kōrin, *Red and White Plum Blossoms (Kōhakubai-zu byōbu)*. MOA Museum of Art.

tric compositions from artists like Degas and Toulouse-Lautrec. As described in Chapter 4, Monet used the related "trailing branch motif" in his *Water Lilies* series. Monet was no doubt directly influenced by ukiyo-e artists like Harunobu and Hiroshige, but the close-up technique and superb compositions he observed in their work had been perfected long ago by the "wall and screen painters" of the Momoyama period.

In closing, let us consider a masterpiece that combines all of the above-mentioned ideas: Ogata Kōrin's *Red and White Plum Blossoms (Kōhakubai-zu byōbu)*. This screen's rich golden field exemplifies Japan's "principle of ornamentation" with great refinement, but it also displays a range of other characteristics of Japanese art.

First, although this is a dazzlingly ornamental work, the pictorial space is far from filled by its subjects. Kōrin depicts only two plum trees and the river that flows between them. There is no ground, no sky, nothing else at all to flesh out the environment. Second, the trees are depicted as if viewed from the side, but the central river flows from the top of the painting to the bottom, meaning that it is viewed from above. Multiple points of view coexist in the work despite there being only a handful of subjects. And third, the white plum tree on the left is shown rising from its roots, curving left out of the frame, and then curving once more to reenter from the top: a fine example of the aesthetics of the close-up. Other elements combining both ornamentation and Japanese sensibilities include the highly stylized ripples on the river (one of Chesneau's "pictorial effects") and the seasonality of the subjects.

Finally, let it not be overlooked that, like many other examples in this chapter, *Red and White Plum Blossoms* was painted on a screen. It was meant to be part of an interior space, an adornment for everyday life. In the age of *japonisme*, too, European artists discovered the Japanese sense of beauty not only in paintings but in handcrafts meant for daily use. We might call this a manifestation of the distinctly Japanese capacity for creating beauty where aesthetic expression meets everyday life.

Part II

EAST–WEST ENCOUNTERS

7. East and West in Meiji Painting

In the history of Japanese art in the Meiji period, Paris came to play an important role in 1896. This was the year the Tokyo Fine Arts School opened its Department of Western Painting headed by Kuroda Seiki, who had spent nearly a decade in France before returning to Japan three years earlier. Kuroda was not the first Japanese painter to study in France, of course; starting in the late 1870s, many had made the journey, from Yamamoto Hōsui and Goseda Yoshimatsu (who arrived in Paris in 1878 and 1880 respectively) to Hyakutake Kaneyuki, Kawamura Kiyoo, Gōda Kiyoshi, and Fuji Masazō. Some stayed longer than others, but all were serious about honing their craft. Goseda and Fuji even had works selected for exhibition at the renowned Salon, an honor difficult even for French painters to achieve.[1] With the exception of Fuji, who went from France straight to the United States and never set foot in Japan again, all of these painters returned to Japan before Kuroda, but their subsequent influence was minimal. One reason for this is that they had spent their time in Paris studying under Academic painters of the old generation, like Jean-Léon Gérôme and Léon Bonnat; their accomplishments lacked the luster of the new. Another, more important reason is that, when they returned to Japan in the 1880s, they found the country in the grip of a particularly strong resurgence of the traditional arts. Western-style painting by Japanese artists, called *yōga*, was banished from the public art school curriculum, and opportunities to exhibit such works publicly were snatched away. The French-trained returnees—not to mention those who had studied in Germany, Italy, or England—had nowhere to display their abilities.

Compared to his predecessors, Kuroda was doubly fortunate. Because he started his art training in Paris slightly later, he was able to study under Raphaël Collin, who, while still of the Academic tradition, at least belonged to the new generation influenced by the Impressionists. When Kuroda returned to Japan, the importance of once-rejected *yōga* was again being recognized. Moreover, Kuroda was the scion of a distinguished family from the Satsuma domain, which had helped to establish the new Meiji government. His adoptive father (and biological uncle) Kuroda Kiyotsuna had contributed to the Meiji Restoration and received a high rank in the new bureaucracy. Kuroda thus enjoyed a combination of superior talent and good fortune that made him a central figure in the Japanese art world almost as soon as he returned from France, and a mentor and guide for many years thereafter.

To understand Kuroda's place in the story of modern Japanese art, however, we must look even further back and consider the history and principles underlying the introduction of Western art in the first thirty years of the Meiji period.

The Technical Fine Arts School and Westernization

In terms of Japanese art history, the period from 1868 to 1896—the first two-thirds of the Meiji era—divides neatly into two separate halves around the year 1882. The first period was characterized by a spirit of thoroughgoing Westernization in the name of "enlightenment and civilization" (*bunmei kaika*). Japan's traditional values were rejected, and Western art became the absolute model. The second period was precisely the opposite: backlash against rapid Westernization fueled movements to revive tradition that prized *nihonga*, as Japanese-style paintings were called, over the Westernized *yōga*, which were suppressed. As symbols of these utterly opposed extremes, the first period is represented by the Technical Fine Arts School (Kōbu Bijutsu Gakkō), and the second by the Tokyo Fine Arts School (Tōkyō Bijutsu Gakkō).

The Technical Fine Arts School opened on the campus of the Imperial College of Engineering in Toranomon, Tokyo, on November 6, 1876. The *Kōbushō enkaku hōkoku* (Historical report of the Ministry of Public Works), published in 1889, describes the event in subdued terms:

> November 6. Technical Fine Arts School established, attached to the
> main college. The school has two departments: Painting and Sculp-
> ture. The first will teach painting methods and oils, while the second
> will teach a range of techniques for creating various forms from
> plaster. It has three Italian professors and its regulations have been
> established and promulgated.

Thus was born Japan's first public school of fine arts. Compare this to the introduction of Western music: the Music Investigation Committee (Ongaku Torishirabe-gakari), predecessor to the Tokyo Music School, was not formed until 1879, and its first three teachers, led by Luther W. Mason, did not arrive from Boston until the following year.

This does not necessarily mean that the Meiji government valued art more than music. Rather, it shows that, in the early Meiji period, painting was considered a *technology* rather than an art form. Indeed, the goal of the Technical Fine Arts School, as stated in its regulations, was "to transfer the *techniques* of the modern West to the existing profession [of art] in our nation of Japan and thus be of assistance to the various trades." (Emphasis added.)

Above all, however, the fact that the Music Investigation Committee was an organ of the Ministry of Education, while the Technical Fine Arts School was under the Ministry of Public Works, clearly shows their different philosophical underpinnings. The Imperial College of Engineering had since its founding sought to "encourage the greater development of engineering," and the subjects it taught covered the full range of useful and practical skills, including civil and mechanical engineering, telegraphy, architecture, chemistry, and mining. Its purpose was to introduce the latest Western technological culture under the principles of "civilization and enlightenment" and "promotion of industry." Art played a supporting role at best.

Given this perspective, it is no surprise that the Technical Fine Arts School was clearly inclined toward Western painting from the start. The Music Investigation Committee had separate departments for Western and Japanese music, but the Technical Fine Arts School's two departments (painting and sculpture) both taught Western techniques. The traditional arts of Japan were completely absent, although this was less a conscious exclusion than a result of the fact that the school's founders, from Minister of Public Works Itō Hirobumi on down, simply did not think of the term "fine arts" as including the Kanō school of painting or the Buddhist sculpture of the Edo period.

Indeed, the Imperial College of Engineering was founded on principles of comprehensive Westernization. Its own original regulations required that (1) "Westerners be selected for all teaching positions" and (2) "dress, diet, and abode all be in the Western style." The impracticality of this vision so soon after the Meiji Restoration did result in the regulations being rewritten a year or so later, but the dizzying pace of change conveys a palpable sense of the desire, even the impatience, for Westernization among the leaders of the new age. The Technical Fine Arts School was above all a product of that results-oriented Westernizing philosophy.

The idea of painting as a technology had actually arisen many decades earlier, among the Japanese artists who encountered Western art toward the end of the eighteenth century. Notwithstanding the "national isolation" of the Edo period, some contact with the West did occur, and the rare and exotic cultural goods that entered Japan through the trading port of Nagasaki fascinated the era's progressive intellectuals. The *Kaitai shinsho* (New book of anatomy), a 1774 translation of a Dutch book on anatomy, was one of the most brilliant products of this fascination.

Most of the art imported to Japan in this period consisted of copperplate prints and illustrations in books, but this was enough to convey the essential characteristics of Western art. What astonished Japanese artists most were the Western techniques for accurately reproducing the outer world just as it appeared to the eye. Satake Shozan, head of the Akita domain (home of Odano Naotake, illustrator of the *Kaitai shinsho*) was an accomplished artist and theorist in his own right. In his *Gahō kōryō* (Manifesto on artistic technique), written in 1778, he proudly declared that, while traditional Japanese drawing techniques did not distinguish between a sphere and a circle or tell viewers whether boats drifting on a river were near or far, he had mastered Western techniques for clearly depicting these differences. Shiba Kōkan's *Seiyō gadan* (Discussion of Western art), published two decades later in 1799, expresses the same ideas in similar terms:

> It is impossible to depict the truth with Japanese and Chinese techniques. When depicting something rounded, the artist draws a circle and calls it a bullet. The swelling at its center cannot be shown. In a frontal portrait, the artist cannot depict the central prominence of the nose.

The goal of painting was to "depict the truth," and Western techniques were far better suited to this than Japanese or Chinese ones: Kōkan expresses these ideas quite clearly. This mode of thinking was passed down through Takahashi Yuichi, the most important *yōga* painter of the late Edo and early Meiji period, to the students at the Technical Fine Arts School. The extreme emphasis on reproducing three-dimensional space through depictions of depth and "protrusions" set the tone in many ways for the subsequent reception of Western art in Japan. The specific techniques involved were those perfected during the Renaissance: perspective, shading, and modeling. In the West, these techniques were intimately bound up with classical aesthetic theory, but *yōga* painters in Japan showed little interest in the fundamental aesthetics underlying Western painting. They only wished to extract and import the techniques that had developed as a result. Antonio Fontanesi, one of the "three Italians" who taught at the Technical Fine Arts School, did in fact discuss principles of beauty in his lectures, but his aesthetic philosophy was lost on his Japanese students. For them, Western painting was above all a technology for realistic pictorial reproduction.

This practical focus of the first government art school in Japan—that is, its view of art as technology—strongly influenced the development of Western-style art in Japan in both positive and negative ways. On one hand, the emphasis on applied technique made it possible to receive a formal artistic education under distinguished Western teachers very soon after the Meiji Restoration. Without this impetus, *yōga* painters would have spent much longer groping in the dark. On the other hand, we must admit that prioritizing technique left painting unable to maintain its independence as an art form. There was no room to cultivate the kind of aesthetic principles that underpin artistic activity. When Ernest Fenollosa used his own aesthetics as a weapon against *yōga* in the 1880s, the Technical Fine Art School could offer no aesthetic or artistic principle strong enough to defend against the attack. Out of step with the times, it ultimately closed its doors.

The Tokyo Fine Arts School and the Traditionalist Revival

In contrast with the Technical Fine Arts School, which enlisted the help of Italy's government to find Italian teachers in time for its opening, the establishment of the Tokyo Fine Arts School was driven by a single American with a passion for Japanese art: Harvard-educated Ernest Fenollosa. Fenollosa came to Japan to teach at the University of Tokyo in 1878, coincidentally entering Japan just as Fontanesi, who by then had completed his two-year engagement at the Technical Fine Arts School, was leaving. At the University of Tokyo, Fenollosa taught political science, but he had also studied oil painting and sketching in Boston and was deeply interested in art. Naturally, he knew almost nothing of Japanese art on his arrival, and initially had plans to promote Western art in Japan, even discussing the matter with prominent *yōga* painter Takahashi Yuichi. According to Yuichi's papers, the two of them became friendly around 1880 and planned a lecture series to bring *yōga* to wider attention, but these plans fell by the wayside when Fenollosa's interest turned toward Japanese art instead.[2]

The initial catalyst for this change was Fenollosa's awakening to the beauty of antique Japanese artwork on frequent visits to Nara and Kyoto. As well as beauty, he saw in these works the living pulse of Greco-Buddhist art[3] and even echoes of the art of ancient Greece and Rome, which shocked him greatly. From this discovery, he framed a historical view that saw Japan's traditional arts as having been nourished by the stream of ancient Greek

Classicism. He found the results highly praiseworthy, viewing the Kanō School in particular as inheritors of this Classicism in its most authentic form, and set about working to help effect a revival of these traditions. His evaluations of Japanese painting were based not on mere exoticism but instead rooted in his distinctive, clear historical consciousness and aesthetic sensibilities. For example, he was highly critical of the "literati paintings" (*bunjinga*) then popular in Japan, stating in a well-known 1882 lecture that "true painting is currently being crushed by literati paintings on one side and oils on the other."

In order to revive this "true painting," he established an art association in 1884 to sponsor lectures and exhibit and appraise antique artwork. He also sought out contemporary *nihonga* painters like Kanō Hōgai and Hashimoto Gahō to offer his assistance. Finally, with the help of his student and kindred spirit Okakura (Kakuzō) Tenshin, his passion for reviving traditional art culminated in the establishment of the Tokyo Fine Arts School in 1887.

This was just four years after the closure of the Technical Fine Arts School in 1883, which shows how greatly the Meiji government's thinking on art education had changed in that short period. If the Technical Fine Arts School had embodied a comprehensive impulse toward Westernization, the Tokyo Fine Arts School was its exact opposite, focused entirely on reviving tradition. Fenollosa and Okakura spent the year before its establishment touring art schools across Europe, but in all their travels found "nothing that should be adopted in Japan."

The Tokyo Fine Arts School trained artists in three fields: painting, sculpture, and crafts. Only traditional Japanese techniques were taught; Western methods like oil painting and sketching with pencils were completely excluded. In the classrooms, students kneeled on tatami mats with neither chairs nor easels. Even the uniforms worn by teachers and students, designed by Okakura, were based on formal attire from the Nara period. Arts policy had gone from one extreme to the other, from radical Westernization to steadfast traditionalism, in less than two decades.

The traditionalism of the Tokyo Fine Arts School was not, however, mere nostalgia; it also sought to create "new *nihonga*." Having discovered the inheritors of ancient Greek Classicism in the antique art of Japan, Fenollosa now anticipated the birth of a contemporary *nihonga* making full use of that tradition. Okakura, who took a broader, more international approach, lectured on the incorporation into *nihonga* of Western-style expressions of space and light. The young painters who studied under Okakura, including Yokoyama Taikan, Hishida Shunsō, and Shimomura Kanzan, embarked on a bold exploration of new worlds of expression, hitherto unknown to traditional art—and this very novelty would, in time, place them in firm opposition to the conservative school within *nihonga*.

Meanwhile, the momentum of the traditionalist revival left *yōga* painters in an increasingly difficult position. Following the closure of the Technical Fine Arts School, no remaining public institution taught Western painting techniques. Private schools were losing so many students that some were forced to close their doors. *Yōga* were not even welcome at the National Painting Fair held by the government in 1884 to promote the fine arts. The opposition to *yōga* was reminiscent of the "expel the barbarians" movement in the last days of the shogunate, and many *yōga* painters would later recall being persecuted like enemies of the nation. To push back, a group of *yōga* painters gathered around former students of Fontanesi, like Asai Chū and Koyama Shōtarō, to form the Meiji Fine Arts Society in 1889. The society's paintings gradually came to be accepted by more exhibitions, but the world of *yōga* did not retain its former vitality until a new figure entered the story. That figure was Kuroda Seiki.

Kuroda Seiki and the New School

Kuroda returned from his nine-year stay in France in 1893. Three years later, he was appointed head of the Tokyo Fine Arts School's newly created Western painting department. In the same year, he also left the Meiji Fine Arts Society—of which he had been a member since his return to Japan—and formed the White Horse Society (Hakuba-kai). The White Horse Society also counted among its members Kume Keiichirō, who had been friendly with Kuroda since they were in Paris together. With the society's first exhibition, Kuroda began a period of dazzling activity in both the public and private spheres.

Kuroda's impetus for leaving the Meiji Fine Arts Society and creating his own was the difference between the style he had learned in Paris, influenced by the Impressionists and distinguished by its use of bright colors, and that of the inheritors of Fontanesi's approach who made up the rest of the Meiji Fine Arts Society. Kuroda's teacher Raphaël Collin was an Academic painter, but his colors and composition reflected Impressionist influence; his style might be called "Impressionistic Academism." To those accustomed to the dark canvases of the Meiji Fine Arts Society, Kuroda's brightly colored works seemed bizarre. When Kuroda exhibited *Nap* (*Hirune*), painted the year after his return to Japan, at the society's Sixth Art Exhibition, Takayama Chogyū's criticism in the March 1896 edition of the general-interest magazine *Taiyō* (The sun) was biting:

> In the painting, the face and hands are ornamented with arrangements of fine lines in yellow, red, blue, purple, and other colors. It is difficult to tell at a glance whether the form depicted is even human. Perhaps this seemed beautiful to the South School, but the lovers of painting in the society could only exchange baffled looks.

Under the circumstances, Kuroda's decision to break with the Meiji Fine Arts Society and move in a new direction with the White Horse Society seems quite natural. The result was that, starting in 1896, the history of *yōga* is driven by the division and competition between the "New School" of the White Horse Society and the "Old School" of the Meiji Fine Arts Society and its successor the Pacific Painting Association.[4] The rivalry between the schools was much discussed in society. The New School and Old School were also known as the Purple School and the Resin School, based on the types of color palettes they favored, and the South School and the North School, as seen in the quotation from Chogyū above.

In short, the history of the Meiji art world until the mid-1890s was primarily about the struggle between *yōga* and *nihonga*, but Kuroda's arrival resulted in two distinct schools of *yōga* whose rivalry attracted more interest than their opposition to *nihonga*. The New–Old rivalry also reflected how painters were trained in Paris. The White Horse Society counted among its members many disciples of Raphaël Collin, from Kuroda and Kume to successors like Okada Saburōsuke and Wada Eisaku, while the core membership of the Meiji Fine Arts Society and Pacific Painting Association had mostly trained in the atelier of Jean-Paul Laurens, a noted traditionalist even within the Academy. The two schools of *yōga* thus reflected two inclinations within Academism, which speaks to how close the relationship between Japan and Paris was at the time.

At the same time, the "new *nihonga*" painters of the Japan Art Institute (Nippon Bijutsuin, established 1898), who had boldly adopted Western forms of expression under the guidance of Okakura Tenshin, were emerging as an opposing force to the more conservative school of *nihonga*. The situation had already moved beyond simple "*yōga* vs. *nihonga*" framing. Both camps were internally divided between old and new, and sometimes the New Schools of *nihonga* and *yōga* even joined forces. Okakura himself was relatively sympathetic toward the "new *yōga*" of Kuroda and Kume, and the White Horse Society's first exhibition was actually held in conjunction with a Japan Art Institute exhibition.

A New Aesthetic Theory

Kuroda brought more to *yōga* than techniques for representing light using vibrant colors. His goal was to transplant to Japan not just the "impressionistic Academism" of Raphaël Collin but also the fundamental principle of Academism that underpinned it: *Ut pictura poesis*, "As painting, so poetry." Paintings were expected not simply to re-create what was visible but to express some kind of idea, philosophy, or story. In the West, this idea became firmly established in the Renaissance, and remained foundational until the nineteenth century. This was why "historical paintings" in the broad sense (that is, including religious, allegorical, and narrative works) were at the very top of the Academy's artistic hierarchy.

As we have seen, however, in Japan from the eighteenth century through the age of the Technical Fine Arts School, Western painting was above all viewed as a set of techniques for representing the three-dimensional world. Aesthetic concerns went unnoticed. Kuroda remedied this by furnishing *yōga* with a new view of painting itself.

The principles underlying Academism became clear to Kuroda before he finished his training in Paris. In a letter to his father dated April 17, 1890, he writes:

> Here [in France], there is a practice of expressing ideas with human figures. For example, among my teacher's paintings, there is one called *Spring* in which a beautiful woman lies stark naked in a flowering field, idly touching a blade of grass to her mouth . . . . Looking at this picture, the ignorant would see nothing but a naked woman lying on the grass . . . and criticize it on foolish grounds such as "Women do not really loll about naked in the fields of Europe." But what my teacher painted was the feeling of spring, and that is why he borrowed the form of a beautiful woman like a flower just coming into bloom. In other words, this spring exists only in the human psyche, and when someone who shares my teacher's sensitivities views it, they feel an inexpressible delight.

In short, Kuroda was well aware that in Academism, painting was about representing the internal world of thought rather than reproducing the external, natural world. The work he refers to is probably Collin's well-known allegorical painting *Floréal*. After returning to Japan, Kuroda experimented with ambitious works like *Tales of Old* (*Mukashigatari*); *Wisdom, Impression, Sentiment* (*Chi, kan, jō*); and *Flowering Field* (*Hanano*) in an attempt to transplant this kind of allegorical and historical painting to Japan. His influence is one of the major reasons so many *yōga* artists painted historical

Raphaël Collin, *Floréal*. The University Art Museum, Tokyo University of the Arts.
Photo: The University Art Museum, Tokyo University of the Arts / DNPartcom

Kuroda Seiki, *Flowering Field*
(*Hanano*). Tokyo National Museum.
Source: ColBase (https://colbase.
nich.go.jp/)

paintings in the last fifteen years of the Meiji period. *Paradise Under the Sea*
(*Wadatsumi no iroko no miya*) by prominent White Horse Society member
Aoki Shigeru is one of the most accomplished works in this vein.

However, what Kuroda viewed as historical painting—work that narrated
a philosophy or principle—failed to flourish in the *yōga* world thereafter.
The stubborn persistence of *yōga*'s initial realist bent and emphasis on technique was one factor. It must also be admitted that, superb as Kuroda's technique was, he was not blessed with the imaginative powers needed to conceive

Aoki Shigeru, *Paradise Under the Sea* (*Wadatsumi no iroko no miya*). Artizon Museum, Ishibashi Foundation.

of historical paintings. The decisive reason, however, was that the principles of Academism were already beginning to collapse in the West. At the end of the nineteenth century, when Paris had become the art center of the world, the Academy was still a powerful force, but avant-garde outsiders like Manet and the Impressionists had redirected the artistic mainstream. *Ut pictura poesis* was disavowed. Historical paintings became a thing of the past. Painting was about to embark on its twentieth-century adventure into new forms of expression. Kuroda was struggling to introduce the long-held principles of the Academy to Japan just as those principles were about to vanish in the West.

However, as we have already seen in the case of Raphaël Collin, Academic painting itself was changing. Collin was influenced by more than just the colors of the Impressionists. His outdoor scenes like *Floréal* and *Garden Corner* (*Coin de jardin*) are drawn with high horizons and barely any sky, with the human figures viewed from above. Compositional techniques of this sort were favored by Gauguin and the painters known as the Nabis; they broke with traditional expectations, dating to the Renaissance, that paintings should take an eye-level perspective, and eventually led to the flattening of the picture. Intriguingly, both the bright colors of the Impressionists and the bird's-eye view of Gauguin and the Nabis were largely inspired by ukiyo-e prints and other Japanese art.

Kuroda did not realize it, but when he faithfully upheld his teacher's style in works like *Nap* and *Flowering Field*, he was in fact incorporating characteristic elements of Edo-period art that had ridden the wave of *japonisme* to Europe, been adopted into Collin's Academism, and then returned to Japan.

A mere half-century after Japan reopened to the outside world, the distance between it and Europe had already shrunk enough to make this kind of mutual influencing and exchange possible. When the Meiji period ended and the Taishō period began, this distance would shrink even further, with new artistic movements centered around Paris quickly inspiring a response in Japan and becoming important factors in the history of twentieth-century Japanese art.

Notes

1. Goseda Yoshimatsu's work was selected by the Salon in 1881, 1882, and 1883. Fuji Masazō's was selected in 1888.

2. The Takahashi Yuichi Papers on Oil Painting (*Takahashi Yuichi aburae shiryō*) in the collection of Tokyo University of the Arts contain the following passage: "In Meiji 13 [1880], the Ministry of Education's 'hired American' (*oyatoi beikokujin*) Fenollosa came to Yuichi's residence at [the private school] Tenkai Gakusha and spoke of his position on the promotion of Western painting. He also paid many visits to the Department of Painting and discussed the possibility of lecturing on Western painting and its history to the department's students and general audiences. Yuichi agreed to engage his services for lectures. After this, Yuichi sometimes visited Fenollosa's residence in Hongō, where Fenollosa showed Yuichi his own oil paintings and even gifted him a landscape. After that, their friendship deepened through further discussion of Western painting, but . . . [eventually] Fenollosa's position changed to one of encouraging Japanese painting, and the agreement mentioned above was cancelled."

3. In Fenollosa's late work *Epochs of Chinese and Japanese Art* (1912), the chapter on the Nara and Heian periods is titled "Greco-Buddhist Art in Japan," referring to the artistic synthesis between Hellenistic and Buddhist culture in ancient Bactria and the Indian subcontinent.

4. The Meiji Fine Arts Society dissolved in 1901, overwhelmed by the momentum of the White Horse Society. The following year, Koyama Shōtarō's students Mitsutani Kunishirō, Yoshida Hiroshi, and Nakagawa Hachirō became the core of a group that formed the Pacific Painting Association. Kanokogi Takeshirō and Nakamura Fusetsu, among others, later joined the association.

8. The Avant-Garde in Japanese Art

The history of Japan's avant-garde art movement begins around 1910 and spans some six decades. Superficially, it may appear nothing more than a delayed and sometimes distorted echo of artistic currents in Europe. The very idea of an "avant-garde" was imported from the West, and it is difficult to imagine Futurism or Surrealism in Japan without Western precedents. Japanese avant-garde pioneer Yorozu Tetsugorō himself allowed that in painting his extraordinarily powerful 1911 work *Nude Beauty* (*Ratai bijin*) at the age of twenty-seven, he was "inspired by Van Gogh and Matisse," known to him through reproductions of their work. When David Burliuk, friend to Kandinsky and Larionov, came to Japan in 1920 bearing hundreds of Russian Futurist works, the event provided such a strong and immediate stimulus to the Futurist Art Society that the society reorganized itself, resulting in the birth of the Sanka Independent group. Stylistically, too, Burliuk was hugely influential on Japan's youthful avant-garde painters: compare *The Art of Dostoevsky* (1923) to Kanbara Tai's *On Scriabin's "Poem of Ecstasy"* (*Sukuriabin no "ekusutashii no shi" ni daisu*, 1924). On the theoretical side, Burliuk coauthored a 1923 book with Kinoshita Shūichirō entitled *Mirai-ha to wa? Kotaeru* (What is Futurism? We answer), in which the two describe in detail not only Futurism but also Cubism, Expressonism, the Metaphysical painters, Dadaism, Suprematism, and Orphism. Poet Kitagawa Fuyuhiko's 1929 translation of André Breton's *Manifeste du surréalisme* (1924), followed by the return of painter Fukuzawa Ichirō from a seven-year sojourn in France in 1931, sparked interest in Surrealism among many radical young artists in the early 1930s, including the painters Koga Harue, Migishi Kōtarō, and Kitawaki Noboru.

Thus, like many other fields of endeavor in modern Japan, the artistic avant-garde was heavily influenced by close contact with the Western world.

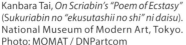

Kanbara Tai, *On Scriabin's "Poem of Ecstasy"* (*Sukuriabin no "ekusutashii no shi" ni daisu*). National Museum of Modern Art, Tokyo. Photo: MOMAT / DNPartcom

David Burliuk, *The Art of Dostoevsky*.

However, that contact is not the only key required to understand avant-garde art in Japan. To reduce six decades of diverse and complex activity to "an imitation of Western models," as some have done, is simplistic, incomplete, and as outdated as trying to explain the French School of Fontainebleau purely in terms of Italian influence. Art historians have noted the importance of traditional Japanese sensibilities in the work of "orthodox" *yōga* painters like Kuroda Seiki and Fujishima Takeji, inspiring a reevaluation of modern Japanese art history from a new perspective.

Unfortunately, much of the early avant-garde's legacy, particularly the "first wave" of the 1910s and 1920s, did not survive later political movements and the chaos of war. The loss of countless works and the vagaries of human memory mean that too much has been forgotten. Nevertheless, for the past quarter-century, many researchers in Japan and elsewhere have engaged in foundational research, discovering forgotten artworks, examining new sources, and tracing historical facts. Although these efforts are ongoing, they have already borne fruit. The time is ripe for a reassessment of the history of the Japanese avant-garde, which owes its richness to a complex combination of imitation with masterful reception, skillful application, occasional resistance, and even true creation.

The Groundswell of Artistic Innovation

To foster our individual art, each of us follows our own path. If a common reason must be found for the establishment of this group and the holding of its first exhibition, seek it nowhere else but in the passion and joy of a group of young men who love and respect each other and, for the sake of the spirit of the coming age, mean to step forward as the avant-garde.

This passage from Kanbara Tai's manifesto for the first exhibition of the avant-garde group Action in 1923 is a fascinating testament to the revolutionary spirit of the age. Two points in particular stand out. First, in a period where the term "avant-garde" was not yet in common use, revolutionary young artists (Kanbara was just twenty-four when he wrote the manifesto in 1922) consciously opposed themselves to the "Exhibition Academism" that was increasingly evident at the Bunten and other imperial exhibitions. The same stance was conveyed in even fierier tones in a manifesto Kanbara Tai had released on the occasion of a personal exhibition several years earlier. In this "Kanbara Tai Manifesto," the young painter insisted that art must be "absolutely free" and declared that "no value can be acknowledged in Academism of any kind." This openly defiant attitude was not limited to Kanbara, or even to his kindred spirits in Action, which lasted just two years. For example, in "Sankaten no Mirai-ha" (Futurism at the Sanka Exhibition), published in the December 1922 edition of *Chūō bijutsu*, Shibuya Osamu described Futurism as a movement of "no moldy stagnation . . . or past . . . only progress, destruction, creation." In the April 1923 issue of the same magazine, Murayama Tomoyoshi, who had just returned from Germany to become a central figure in the formation of the MAVO group, expressed similar sentiments in an essay titled "Sugiyuku hyōgen-ha: Ishikiteki kōseishugi e no joronteki dōnyū" (The passing of expressionism:

A preliminary introduction to conscious constructivism). Yearning for revolution was clearly widespread among the young artists of the age.

The second noteworthy feature of the Action manifesto is its embrace of two important elements of avant-garde art: individuality ("each of us follows our own path") and a craving for the new ("for the sake of the spirit of the coming age"). These two elements might be called the fundamental principles of all Japanese avant-garde movements at the time. This is evident from countless contemporary manifestos, critical essays, and introductions to exhibitions, which inevitably proclaim the fall of past aesthetics and hail the creative freedom that will take their place. Common guidelines and principles for judging artistic value were no more. The only standards now were originality, creativity, and self-expression: an individualistic aesthetic widely embraced in the art world at the time. Natsume Sōseki, for example, wrote a review of the sixth Bunten exhibition for the *Tokyo Asahi Shinbun* in 1912 that flatly states, "Art begins with self-expression and ends with self-expression."

These two elements were, of course, inherent in European avant-garde movements as well, but their rise to prominence had special meaning in Japan in light of historical circumstance. In the West, individualistic aesthetics and the search for creativity were born with Romanticism and came to be strongly emphasized as the nineteenth century progressed. In a way, these were the fundamental principles that set the course of modern art. Things were different in Japan. As I detailed in the previous chapter, from the late Edo period to the end of the nineteenth century, Western painting was above all viewed as a set of techniques for faithfully reproducing what was visible to the eye. *Yōga* painters believed that the chief goal of art was to accurately reflect the world, and because Western techniques of perspective, shading, and modeling brought that goal within reach—made it possible to "distinguish a circle from a sphere," as Shiba Kōkan put it—they were superior to Japanese and Chinese methods. However, as the nineteenth century gave way to the twentieth, a new way of thinking appeared that emphasized self-expression over accurate reflection. The rapid spread of this idea created an intellectual and cultural climate that would later support the avant-garde movement.

The Intellectual Climate of 1900

This turning point in artistic thought is highly meaningful in the context of Japan's intellectual history. Before we pick up that trail, however, let us quickly review the history of Japanese–European contact in the field of art.

We need not look as far back as the arrival of the first European missionaries in the sixteenth century, but we should not forget that the fervent efforts of eighteenth-century intellectuals like Shiba Kōkan paved the way for the "modernization" of the Meiji period. Even during the age of "national isolation" (*sakoku*), Western thought and knowledge continued to enter Japan through the port at Nagasaki. The information and artifacts that arrived were enormously influential in creating the image of a rational Western world with superior technology, and this view of the West only grew stronger after Japan's "opening" in the mid-nineteenth century.

Once European painting, too, became reasonably widely known, people were fascinated by its ability to depict the visible world accurately. As described in the previous chapter, from 1876 to 1883, the Ministry of Public Works ran a Technical Fine Arts School at which Fontanesi and other Italian instructors taught exclusively Western techniques of painting and sculpture. This, however, was followed by the Tokyo Fine Arts School, which was established in 1887 at the urging of Ernest Fenollosa and his student Okakura (Kakuzō) Tenshin amid a rising tide of classical revivalism and only taught traditional Japanese techniques. Western painting was only added to its curriculum in 1896, when a *yōga* department was created with Kuroda Seiki as its head.

The point of interest here is that Kuroda's arrival coincided with the introduction of new knowledge about Europe's many contemporary art movements. While somewhat influenced by Romanticism, these movements culminated in the subjectivist tide of the 1890s. Through Symbolism, Art Nouveau, and other fin-de-siècle artistic movements tinged by late

Romanticism, the Japanese came to know a more complex and "modern" Western world where rationalism was not necessarily the highest principle. Even Kuroda's "impressionistic Academism" was soon deemed a "New School" in rivalry with the "Old School" faithful to Fontanesi's teachings. In a 1901 essay titled "Geikai tawagoto" (Idle chat about the art world), critic and journalist Iwamura Tōru (a friend of Kuroda's) observes that "if one tallies up the various *isms* sprinkled throughout recent books on art, the number is quite considerable." As examples, Iwamura lists "Classicism, Medievalism, Modernism, Romanticism, Impressionism, Symbolism, Pointillism, Pleinairism, Rosicrucianism, Pre-Raphaelism, Ruskinism, Tolstoyism," and more. The idea of the Western world as a unified, rational whole was disassembled, and realistic reproduction was cast aside in favor of self-worship.

Perhaps the best indicator of the intellectual and artistic climate at the turn of the century is Takayama Chogyū's 1901 essay "Biteki seikatsu o ronzu" (On living artistically). Chogyū, a highly popular critic at the time, argues that the greatest human joy is to be found in "living artistically," which for him meant distancing oneself from "the compulsions and duties of society" and seeking that life "in the kingdom of your own breast."

This is even more intriguing in light of an 1895 essay by Chogyū called "Dōtoku no risō o ronzu" (On the ideal of virtue). In this work, Chogyū claims that "society is best characterized not as an assembly of individuals but as a unified, virtuous group. . . . The whole has a life and character not to be found in the individual members. To uplift this character and promote this life is the final objective of each individual member." Chogyū's thinking had changed so greatly in the intervening six years that we might even call it a conversion.

A similar change can be seen in the thinking of poet Masaoka Shiki, a contemporary of Chogyū's. In 1895, Shiki was still able to believe in the commonality of many kinds of art. His *Haiku taiyō* (Overview of haiku) published that year includes a passage to that effect:

> Haiku are part of literature, and literature is part of art. Therefore . . .
> painting and sculpture and music and theater and poetry and fiction
> should all be assessed based on the same standards.

However, after fierce debate with poet Yosano Tekkan, a forceful propo-
nent of autolatry, Shiki changed his mind. In his sickbed diaries published in
1901 as *Bokujū itteki* (A drop of ink), he says, with apparent pain, that this
kind of artistic commonality is no longer possible:

> Our tanka [i.e., Tekkan's and Shiki's] have utterly different stan-
> dards. . . . No one speaks of Tekkan and Shiki together.

At around the same time, Tekkan's New Poetry Society (Shinshisha) was
printing "We strive together to create poetry of the self" as the motto on every copy of the society's journal *Myōjō* (Bright star).

In this context, it is not surprising that poet and sculptor Takamura
Kōtarō defended the "absolute freedom" of artists in his renowned 1910 essay "Midori-iro no taiyō" (A green sun). "If two or three people paint a green
sun, I will not say it is not so," writes Kōtarō. "At times it may look that way
to me as well." The essay has been called an "Expressionist manifesto" for
Japan. It hinted at the new direction in which painting would soon pro-
ceed—but note how far such views already were from Takahashi Yuichi's
belief in "faithful reproduction."

As extreme as these individualist sentiments were at times, the will to
artistic revolution was no less powerful. Shimazaki Tōson proudly declared
in the famous preface to his 1904 *Tōson shishū* (Tōson anthology of poetry)
that "the time for new poetry is come at last," and indeed both artists and
poets were champions of the new in this period. The extent of this desire
for revolution is evident in the constant promotion of novelty on the covers
of the many literary magazines founded during the period—even those
that were extremely short-lived. Examples include *Shinsei* (New voices,
founded 1896), *Shinbungei* (New literature, 1901), *Bijutsu shinpō* (Art couri-

er, 1902), *Shinchō* (New tide, 1904—a relaunch of *Shinsei* under a new name), *Shinshichō* (New tides of thought, 1907), and *Shintenchi* (New worlds, 1908). Aoki Shigeru captured the mood of the age well in his 1907 observation that "forty years after the revolution in material systems, the revolution in intellectual nourishment is finally on its way." (Aoki himself was twenty-five at the time.) The ground had finally been prepared for avant-garde artistic movements as we know them today.

Diversity in the Avant-Garde

One distinguishing feature of the Taishō era and the first fifteen years of the Showa era (roughly 1912–1940) is the formation of numerous "outsider" artists' groups (not to be confused with the later usage of "outsider art," dating from the 1970s, as an equivalent to *art brut*). Some of these played an important role in the development of modern art in Japan, such as the Nika Society (Nika-kai, founded 1914) and the Independent Art Association (Dokuritsu Bijutsu Kyōkai, founded 1930). These groups differed in many ways, but shared a clearly expressed desire to pursue independent activities away from government control. They were driven to this by the so-called Bunten (Monbushō Bijutsu Tenrankai, "Ministry of Education Art Exhibition," founded 1907), which sought to bring together artists of every disposition, New and Old School, under one roof—but, as a government-sponsored exhibition, inevitably exhibited a tendency toward Academism. One point in the Nika Society's bylaws makes the intentions of these outsider groups quite clear: "Any person may exhibit what they wish at our exhibitions, but anyone who also seeks to exhibit with the Ministry of Education will be rejected."

Much as the French painters who held a group exhibition in 1874 and were labeled "Impressionists" were of various kinds, participants in the Nika Society's early exhibitions were a diverse group whose only real commonality was their opposition to Bunten. However, because these exhibitions made plenty of room for "anti-naturalistic" artists (as they were called at the time), this outsider group became the stage on which the avant-garde art movement took shape. This is evident from the presence at Nika Society exhibitions of early, experimental work by artists like Tōgō Seiji, Yorozu Tetsugorō, and Kanbara Tai, along with key works by Koga Harue—and the fact that the Nika Society exhibition of 1938 featured artists who were later active in the field of postwar abstract painting, including Yamaguchi Takeo, Yoshihara Jirō, and Saitō Yoshishige. In fact, these three and others formed the famous Room Nine Society (Kyūshitsu-kai), named after the room they shared at the exhibition. The Independent Art Association, meanwhile, provided a stage for artists such as Fukuzawa Ichirō, Migishi Kōtarō, and Kitawaki Noboru.

Any number of other outsider artists' groups could also be offered as examples. Abstract and partly abstract painters like Hasegawa Saburō, Murai Masanari, and Yamaguchi Kaoru formed the New Age *Yōga* Exhibition (Shinjidai Yōgaten) in 1934. Three years later, the group re-formed with several additional members as the Free Artists' Society (Jiyū Bijutsuka Kyōkai). The Art and Culture Association (Bijutsu Bunka Kyōkai, founded 1939), had a clear Surrealistic bent. After the Second World War, and particularly from the mid-1950s onward, avant-garde art movements became even more active and diverse: there was the Gutai ("Concrete") group, followed slightly later by the Neo-Dada Organizers, as well as the Yomiuri Independent Exhibition (Yomiuri Andepandan-ten) on one hand and the Mono-ha ("Thing School") on the other. Even this brief list of representative examples shows the huge variety of activity that was underway.

These avant-garde exploratory movements, their development driven by surprisingly rich energy and intense curiosity about currents in the Western art world, were a broad and highly complex world in themselves, and cannot be dismissed as the work of mere imitators. What becomes clear from an examination of their activities, and what merits further consideration, is that both congeniality and contrariness existed between Japan and the West. We can, of course, find cases of lopsided and even erroneous understanding due to various historical circumstances. For example, the idea of Futurism was much broader in Japan than in Italy. At the same time, however, we see patterns of active reception and rejection that cannot be the result of historical happenstance. In short, although the Western avant-garde was a constant model for the artists of Japan, they consciously and unconsciously selected only the ideas that suited them, and altered what they did select as necessary. This kind of selection and alteration, even if it was not done with conscious intent, hints at a uniquely Japanese sensibility underlying the entire process. Our task is to clarify and understand the nature of that sensibility.

Avant-Garde and Tradition

In a memorable 1933 essay titled "Matsugo no me" (Final views), the writer Kawabata Yasunari touches on his friendship with Koga Harue, who had died not long before. While emphasizing the close commonality between them, Kawabata superbly characterizes Koga's essence as painter:

> I am seen as an inveterate follower and seeker of new trends, new forms in literature. I am thought of as one who loves novelty and takes an interest in newcomers. Sometimes I even have the honor of being called a "conjurer." If that is so, then there must be some resemblance here to Koga's life as a painter. He strove tirelessly to produce avant-garde work, driven by the desire to play a progressive role, and his apparently ever-changing style meant that there were doubtless those who considered him a "conjurer" like me. . . . Koga strove to include the spirit of modern Western art in his work as well, but the nursery rhyme of Buddhism was a constant stream deep in his heart . . . just as it is in mine. Perhaps the reason for our closeness was the old songs behind our new-looking faces.

This opinion is fully justified in itself, but it is even more interesting in light of the fact that it was written at a time of bold experimentation for Kawabata as the standard-bearer for the New Perceptionists (*shinkankaku-ha*). As is well known, Kawabata eventually found himself more drawn to the world of tradition, and today his works are invariably praised for their traditional sensitivities and "ancient Eastern poetic sentiment" (a phrase Kawabata used in describing Koga).

Koga died at the age of thirty-eight, so he had no opportunity to become more than a "new-looking face" and develop in another direction like his friend. However, if something about his work speaks powerfully to us even now, it is clearly not the submersible or swimsuit-clad young women that so astonished people in his day, or even his compositional technique of throwing apparently unrelated images together on the canvas, which cannot be called novel today. No, what appeals to us above all is Koga's slightly unusual but utterly lucid lyricism. The same lyricism can be found in Kawabata's work; in all probability, it is a constant component of Japanese sensibilities.

Similar observations could be made about the woodblock prints Onchi Kōshirō produced around 1915. These were the first abstract artworks in Japan, and they were clearly influenced by Western predecessors (Kandinsky, or possibly Delauney?)—but at the same time the traditional Japanese sense of beauty is easily identifiable within them. The subdued, refined use of color, favored by both the Heian nobility and art-loving Edoites, and the fine, delicately nuanced gradations of tone, are both aspects of this. The exquisite curves and faint, barely distinguishably bowed lines—ambiguous between straight and curved—are also characteristic of Japanese design. The overall poetic, restrained appeal of the prints, too, is common to Japanese art, and can be seen in the work of painters like Okada Kenzō and Yamaguchi Takeo.

This kind of lyricism, born of extreme refinement and boundless energy, sometimes attains even more plaintive and extreme heights. It is probably no coincidence that during the heyday of abstract painting in the 1950s and 1960s, Japanese painters were particularly drawn to so-called "lyrical" abstraction. In fact, the artists of Japan did not really seem interested in pursuing purely geometric abstraction. Neoplasticism, for example, was particularly poorly received in Japan. This is because the aforementioned lyricism was deeply linked to the naturalistic sentiment that penetrates all of Japanese art. For the Japanese, nature cannot be reduced to the logic of ruler and compass. Nature, like our hearts, has "reasons that reason knows not"

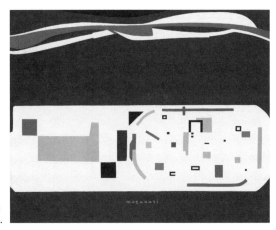

Murai Masanari, *Uruban*.
The Museum of Modern
Art, Kamakura & Hayama.

(as Blaise Pascal put it); even at extremes of artificial refinement, the spiritual side is always valued. One has only to consider the Japanese art of landscaping for proof. This is precisely why Japanese artists prefer natural gestures to geometric ones, and prize the tracks of the hand over ruled lines.

As an example, consider Murai Masanari's *Urban* series. Like the work of the De Stijl group that inspired him, it is made up of squares, rectangles, and straight lines. However, the "straight" lines are not always straight, and the rectangles are not perfect either. It is as if the breath of life has caused the outlines to subtly swell. Respect for nature is also apparent in the handling of stones, sand, and trees by the artists of the Thing School. One even senses in their attitude a connection to the tradition of seeing the sacred in natural elements.

The explorations of the Japanese avant-garde are thus connected to a sense of beauty that has existed in Japan since ancient times. If the diverse and rich fruits of six decades of avant-garde activity have true value in the history of Japanese art, it is because they derive from the passion, intoxication, and tireless effort of artists who came into contact with various Western movements in many different ways—but also from the traditional sensibilities that make Japanese art a valuable part of humanity's heritage.

9. Japanese Academism

When painter Saeki Yūzō visited Maurice de Vlaminck with one of his paintings, Vlaminck's response was scathingly critical: *"Académique!"* Not only was this meeting a major turning point in Saeki's life, it also speaks to how repellent Academism was to the avant-garde artists of the age. By that time, just after the First World War, Vlaminck had abandoned the fierce, explosive colors of his Fauvist period and adopted a much more restrained palette, but he still found Academism an unbearable, despicable thing. In that respect, he was undeniably a child of the modern art movement. For this movement, which began with Courbet and Manet—or, to reach further back, with Romanticism—both rebellion against Academism and rejection *by* Academism were important sources of energy.

In fact, the word "Academism" had always been accompanied by negative connotations. This is clear from the fact that the word came into use not in the seventeenth century, when the French Academy was established, but in the first half of the nineteenth century, when reaction, rejection, and doubts about the Academy had taken vivid form. The first citation for *académisme* in the Larousse *Nouveau dictionnaire étymologique* (1964, fourth edition) is from 1845, in J. B. Richard de Radonvilliers's *Dictionnaire du mots nouveaux*. The word must have been in use to some extent to catch the attention of lexicographers, but if Radonvilliers considered it a neologism, it cannot be much older than his dictionary. It seems safe to suppose that the word *académisme* appeared in the 1840s.

Intriguingly, it was around the same time that the term "avant-garde" was first applied to the new artists' groups that rallied under the banner of opposition to Academism (although, of course, its use as a military term meaning "vanguard" predates this). From this point on, the opposition between "Academism," which maintained major social authority, and "the avant-garde," which rebelled against this authority in search of new forms of artistic expression, would set the tone for modern art. Or, we might say, by rebelling against the Academy's authority, the avant-garde established the notion of "Academism" as the immediate enemy. In other words, the idea of "Academism" always included the sense of a foe to new artistic movements— an opponent to be negated.

We see this dynamic in Courbet's independent exhibition during the 1855 Paris Exposition as a protest against the rejection of several of his paintings from the public exhibition. We also see it in the fact that even as the avant-gardists were barred from the Salon de Paris and thoroughly lambasted—from Manet, who created a scandal at the 1863 Salon des Refusés ("Rejected Exhibition") with the nudity in his *Luncheon on the Grass* (*Le Dejeuner sur les Herbes*), to the Impressionists and Post-Impressionists— they were nevertheless building the history of modern art. In a sense, that history could be called the history of insurrection against Academism.

In recent years, however, a revisionist view of Academism has gained strength—a view seeking to more accurately assess a movement that has long been relegated to the role of villain in modern art history. This is reasonable enough, but it also requires a reevaluation of the Academy itself.

Setting aside the ancient school of philosophers that the word originally referred to, the modern social institution of the Academy was established in seventeenth-century France. Groups of Italian artists in the sixteenth century had also referred to themselves as *accademia*, but it was the Académie royale de peinture et de sculpture, founded in the reign of Louis XIV, the Sun King, that inherited these principles and built an institution that continued to exert significant influence through to the modern age.

The French Academy was the model for the eighteenth-century Royal Academy of Great Britain as well as many other academies in Italy, Germany, and elsewhere. Although it was shut down during the revolutionary period and reopened later in a new form, it effectively survived into the nineteenth century to influence Meiji Japan, so it seems reasonable to identify the seventeenth century as the period when "the Academy" as a universal principle was established. This offers a framework for thinking about similar institutions, such as the Kanō school in Edo-period Japan. Before we embark on these comparisons, however, further analysis of the Western Academy is in order.

Despite differences across nations and time periods, an Academy in the West is fundamentally a social institution for granting awards that is made up of socially accepted artists. It can also be defined by three important features: a system for transmitting technique, an aesthetic philosophy, and a strong historical consciousness.

The first feature is necessary to the Academy as an institution for cultivating artists, and must include a methodology. To provide an education based on clear principles is the Academy's most essential function, which is why the word "Academy" was often adopted by private art schools like the Académie Julian and the Académie Colarossi.

In the case of the French Academy, this function was carried out by an affiliated school. The school's teachers were all members of the Academy, and it enjoyed various special privileges, including the use of nude models—which was not generally permitted at the time—and a system of scholarships that included the Prix de Rome. On one hand, the school unearthed and cultivated much hidden young talent; on the other, it proved useful in centralizing efforts to control the entire art world through dominance of education.

The school's educational methods were founded on drawing. Students began by copying examples, then moved on to the use of plaster and human models in a step-by-step progression from simple to complex. Once they had mastered drawing, students advanced to the oil painting course, which also proceeded step-by-step from depictions of nudes through compositional exercises to practice capturing expressions and gestures, finally arriving at the goal of completing an entire painting. This kind of organized education through fixed methods is common to any Academy.

The second feature of a Western Academy is a clear theory of art and aesthetic philosophy. The French Academy's view of drawing as the cornerstone of art reflected a rationalist philosophy in which forms apprehended by reason were more fundamental than colors appealing to the senses. Its emphasis on theories of perspective, shading, and anatomy was distinctive, but it also had a system of values by which artworks were judged. The most obvious example is the explicit genre hierarchy, which viewed historical paintings (in the general sense that includes scenes from myth and religion) as the highest form, followed by portraits and genre paintings. Landscapes and still lifes were considered lesser works of little value. For example, in the eighteenth century, Jean-Baptiste-Siméon Chardin's still lifes were valued far less than the historical canvases of now-forgotten painters like Jean-Baptiste Pierre and Noël Hallé.

The third feature of Western academies, strong historical consciousness, was related to their theory of art. We might also call it a sense of tradition. The French Academy saw itself as the rightful heir to the finest things since ancient Greece. Indeed, this was a fundamental principle that had supported the Academy since its founding.

A comprehensive educational system, a theory of art, and historical consciousness: these three features not only define the character of Western academies, they are also the fundamental qualifications for applying the term "academy" more generally. If a social institution or structure exhibits these features, it may be called at least a cousin to the academy or Academism. For example, medieval guilds offered a fairly thorough educational system in the form of apprenticeship, but because they lacked a theory of art or historical consciousness, we do not call them "academies."

How does the Kanō School, sometimes referred to as the Academy of Japan, measure up to these conditions?

Founded in the sixteenth century, by the Edo period the Kanō School was certainly a highly developed social institution. Its hereditary nature made it different from comparable Western institutions, but it developed an impressive and expansive network in which every member had his own rank, from the four houses of "inner painters" (*oku-eshi*) and fifteen of "outer painters" (*omote-eshi*) who served the shogun's court, to the various painters who served daimyo across Japan (*goyō-eshi*), and the "town painters" (*machi-*

eshi) with no official position. For the highest-ranking members of this hierarchy, social status and official service as retainers to the shogun or daimyo gave them significant social authority, and with this authority behind them, they played an important role in cultivating new painters—in other words, in art education. Furthermore, the school's educational methods were extremely "Academic," so focused on imitating the finest existing models that they were often criticized as "Copybook-ism" (*funponshugi*). In the eighteenth century, Hayashi Moriatsu, student of Ogata Yūgen, himself a student of Kanō Tan'yū, stated clearly that copying is the most important training method for a painter. The reach of the Kanō educational method can be seen in the number of woodblock-printed books published during this period that were filled with models for imitation, from Moriatsu's own *Gasen* (Net of painting, written 1712 and published 1721) to *Gakō senran* (Deep insight into painterly skill, 1740), a work by an Osaka *machi-eshi* named Ōoka Shunboku who had achieved the impressive rank of *hōgen* in the Kanō school through independent study. Indeed, even artists seen as somewhat heretical, like Itō Jakuchū and Hirose Kinzō of Tosa province, and "Westernists" like *yōga* pioneer Takahashi Yuichi and Kuroda Seiki, began their training using the Kanō school's methods.

What is more, those methods were based on a distinct theory of art. Although influenced in many ways by Chinese art theory, most Edo-era art treatises were written by Kanō school painters. Examples include Kanō Ikkei's *Kōsoshū* (Compendium of painting, 1623), the first Japanese art treatise; Kanō Yasunobu's *Gadō yōketsu* (Secrets of the way of painting, 1680); Kanō Akinobu's *Gadō denju kuketsu* (Secret transmission of the way of painting, 1826); and Asaoka Kōtei's *Koga bikō* (Remarks on ancient paintings, 1845). Previous to this, collections of anecdotes about individual painters and general discussions of artistic topics had been published, but it was the Kanō school that formulated a theory linked to practical results.

In its details, that theory often came very close to Western Academic ideas. For example, the division in Yasunobu's *Gadō yōketsu* between "paintings of quality" (*shitsuga*), born of individual talent, and "paintings of learning" (*gakuga*), which could be achieved through study based on a clear methodology and therefore passed down through the generations, was an Academic principle in itself, as was the corollary idea that "paintings of learning" were therefore more important. Additionally, the way Kanō Seisen'in and other painters of the school adorned the sliding room partitions of Edo Castle was based on a program in which themes were decided based on the purpose of the room—an intriguing parallel to the French Academy's genre hierarchy.

Finally, works like Kanō Ikkei's *Tansei jakubokushū* (Compendium of the saplings of painting, completed ca. 1650) and, above all, Kanō Einō's *Honchō gashi* (History of painting in Japan, 1691) reveal a distinct historical consciousness within the Kanō school. Here, too, Chinese art history provided a model, but Einō's *Honchō gashi*—the first real history of painting in Japan—was more than a recitation of facts. It deployed explicit standards to evaluate the Kanō school as the finest of all the painting schools, demonstrating a historical consciousness connected to self-awareness as upholders of an illustrious tradition. This in itself would be enough reason to call the Kanō school a "Japanese Academy."

The Edo-period Kanō school was thus, in all likelihood, the only organization or social system in Japan before the modern period worthy of the name "Academy." Just like the Western Academy, it had both strengths and weaknesses as a result. The insistence on "Copybook-ist" training in the basics undoubtedly helped maintain a certain standard of technique, but it also contained the ever-present risk of becoming mere formalism. The emphasis on "paintings of learning" safeguarded the wider prosperity of the school and ensured stylistic consistency and efficiency in large-scale collaborative works, but it also tended to suppress outstanding individuality. This inheritance, both good and bad, persisted into the modern period.

Nevertheless, as is the case with Western Academism, the negative view of the Kanō school appears to have been, if anything, too strong in the past. The time has surely come to reassess the Academism of the Kanō school from a more accurate historical perspective.

10. Some Problems of *Japonisme*

— 1 —

What was *japonisme*? At least among those with some connection to art history, there seems to be a commonly agreed-on definition: the entire phenomenon of Japan's influence on Western art in the latter half of the nineteenth century. However, any attempt to define its details more rigorously immediately meets with objections and dissent, and the answers to various questions can differ from expert to expert. For example, should the idea of "Japan's influence" be limited to themes and motifs, or extended to style, or even aesthetics and philosophy? Is a picture of a woman wearing a kimono painted in a completely Western style (there is no shortage of such examples) *japonisme*? Some historians will answer the latter question in the affirmative, while others will disagree, calling it mere exoticism. There are those who hold that the distinctive quality of *japonisme* is daring and sumptuous ornamentation, and others who insist that its essence lies in a purity and simplicity that rejects ornamentation outright. Aubrey Beardsley's refined monochrome line drawings are offered as an example of *japonisme*, but so are works by Van Gogh, whose fierce and dazzling use of color puts him in an utterly different world. The serenely flat fields of mild color preferred by the Nabis are *japonisme*; so is Toulouse-Lautrec's nimble brushwork. So diverse is the range of expression invoked that at a glance it appears to be a miscellany—what exactly do these works have in common? Could it be that *japonisme* is not one thing but several? Should we speak of multiple *japonismes*?

At the same time, the very idea of "influence" is deeply ambiguous and even dangerous. As in all historical research, we risk falling into the *post hoc, ergo propter hoc* fallacy. To postulate a causal relationship between two

Vincent van Gogh, *Flowering Plum Orchard (after Hiroshige)*
(*Bloeiende pruimenboomgaard (naar Hiroshige)*).
Van Gogh Museum. Photo: Bridgeman Images / DNPartcom

forms or styles of expression simply because they resemble each other is highly arbitrary. The validity of such judgments depends not just on the closeness of the resemblance but also on whether historical facts can be found to support them. This requires meticulous analysis of artworks and thorough review of sources. Sometimes, of course, a relationship of influence is self-evident, as when Van Gogh was so captivated by Hiroshige's prints that he made a copy of one in oils. However, even in a case like this, we must consider whether Van Gogh's fervor actually derived from an inner desire to find new solutions to issues inherent to the development of Western art. If so, we cannot explain away this painting simply by calling Van Gogh a lover of Japanese art. On the contrary: alongside outside influence, the historical development of Western art plays an equally important role, so it surely behooves us to place Van Gogh in his proper historical context.

In any case, direct imitation is rare. Most cases of influence are neither direct nor clear, appearing instead as a kind of affinity that resists precise definition. Artworks are by their nature complex and subtle things, and their origins and formative processes cannot be broken down like those of a chemistry experiment. However certain the font of inspiration for a given artwork may seem, its actual source may prove to be entirely different, and even close similarity of expression may be due to coincidence rather than influence. In the history of art, the same cause does not always have the same effect, and similar phenomena do not always derive from the same cause.

In one of the letters Van Gogh wrote from his house in Arles to his brother Theo, the painter writes, "Have you read *Madame Chrysanthème*? It really gave me a lot to think about, that the real Japanese have nothing on their walls. . . . Ah, so that's how you have to look at a *japonaiserie*—in a nice bright room, completely bare, open to the landscape." He continues: "Myself, I work here in a bare interior, 4 white walls and red tiles on the floor" (Letter 509, Van Gogh Museum translation). Van Gogh was obviously influenced by Japanese tastes here. However, it would be a stretch to similarly connect the Japanese model to the fact that today's museum curators display art in ways that give it space to breathe, rather than filling entire walls with paintings in the manner of Hubert Robert's vision for the Louvre's Grand Gallery.

To offer another example of the problem of influence in *japonisme*, there is a lithograph by Toulouse-Lautrec long thought to have been inspired by one of Suzuki Harunobu's *shunga* prints. Michel Melot, however, has made the extremely trenchant observation that it may actually have been based on a contemporary photograph.[1] This is an excellent example of the difficulty of reaching a decisive conclusion about the relationship between two works, irrespective of formal similarities. We should not, for example, rule out the possibility that Toulouse-Lautrec knew *both* of these sources and combined them create a new artistic realm of his own.

Japonisme also faces the problem of mistaken identity. Inventories of furniture and craftwork that "arrived from China" during the reign of Louis XIV sometimes listed goods that were actually Japanese, and the so-called *chinoiserie* of the eighteenth century sometimes included motifs and imagery that really ought to be called *japonaiserie* instead. At the time, those in the West did not always clearly distinguish between China and Japan, and tended to lump everything from the "Far East" together as *chinoiserie*. (Even James Ensor's late nineteenth-century *Still Life with Chinoiseries* includes craftworks that are clearly Japanese). Conversely, when *japonisme* was at its zenith, wallpaper and fabrics for interior decoration included patterns whose subjects were arranged in ways that were considered Japanese but were really more Chinese in nature, or perhaps a compromise between the two.

A stranger but more common example are the items that were definitely made in Japan but stylistically very far from Japanese art, particularly in the late nineteenth century after Japan opened its ports to the West. Most of these items were craftworks made for export to suit Western tastes in Japanese art—or, more accurately, to suit what their Japanese creators *thought* were Western tastes in Japanese art. Like a paper balloon that grows fuller as it is batted back and forth, the idea of Japan traveled back and forth between two worlds, drifting ever further from reality as it swelled into new and unexpected shapes. This back-and-forth exchange of imagery and the sometimes bizarre results it produced are another noteworthy problem posed by *japonisme*.

The diversity of the issues mentioned above reflects the complexity of *japonisme*. Nevertheless, it is difficult to deny that something called *japonisme* did exist, and that the scope of its effects was probably much wider than is typically believed. Unlike *chinoiserie* and Orientalism, *japonisme* was linked to almost every facet of art, from content to form, from style to method, and across media ranging from painting and sculpture to handcrafts, architecture, and photography. Nor was it unrelated to the major changes in aesthetic philosophy and perspectives on art that were occurring in the West at the time. In my opinion, *japonisme* was a wide-ranging, comprehensive movement, and accordingly we must clearly delineate its facets (motifs, techniques, styles, aesthetics, etc.) and measure the degree of its assimilation by each country, age, and even artist, analyzing the background and causes in each case.

Art curator Geneviève Lacambre, in one of her many contributions to the study of *japonisme*, divides France's reception of Japanese art into the following four stages:

> 1. Adoption of Japanese motifs into an eclectic repertoire. This was part of the addition of new decorative motifs from every country and age, without eliminating any.
> 2. Selective copying of exotic (to France) and naturalistic motifs from Japan, with assimilation of the latter at a particularly early stage.
> 3. Imitation of refined Japanese techniques.
> 4. Analysis and application of the principles and methods within Japanese art.[2]

These four stages describe the classic process of reception by one culture of another: discover, adopt, assimilate, create. Notwithstanding certain exceptions and differences of period, degree, and method, the same stages were also evident in countries outside France. Without denying that the idiosyncrasies of individual works are what give art its essential value, this exhibition [*Le japonisme*, 1988, for which this essay was written] aims to clarify this historical process through carefully selected examples.

In the end, the goals and methods of research on *japonisme* are the same as those in other fields of art research. The first task is to establish the facts by surveying, searching, and thoroughly examining the sources, including the artworks themselves. Next we must find the hidden connections between those facts, establish their scope of validity, and locate them historically. The process finally brings us to a greater and deeper understanding of genuine artwork. Naturally, we must also have the humility to accept that creative endeavors of great genius often include a mystical component beyond the ken of others.

— 2 —

Let us begin by retracing the facts.

If we pass over the age of Marco Polo and his fabled "Zipangu" (important as this legend was in implanting in the West the idea of Japan as a "civilized" place "abundant beyond all measure" in gold), the first true contact between Japan and the West took place in 1543, when a Chinese junk with three Portuguese men aboard was forced to land at Tanegashima, a tiny island off the southern coast of Kyushu. Several years later, a group of Portuguese Jesuit missionaries led by Francis Xavier arrived. The reports they sent home gave Europe firsthand information, however imperfect, about the people of the Japanese archipelago.

The relationship between Japan and the West continued without interruption after that point, even after Christianity was banned. Not even the Tokugawa shogunate's policy of near-complete isolation, adopted in 1639, severed ties entirely. During this period, the Dutch maintained a thin trickle of foreign trade as the only Westerners permitted to build a trading house on the artificial island of Dejima in Nagasaki Harbor. The range of activities permitted to the Dutch was strictly limited, but powerful curiosity drove both sides to pursue their exchange of goods and ideas with great fervor, small scale notwithstanding. (Note that during this period, particularly after the eighteenth century, Japan was home to a small but dedicated coterie of "Westernist" intellectuals who sought to learn more about European civilization in spite of their nation's apparent isolation. This has no direct connection to *japonisme*, of course, but neither is it entirely unrelated. The efforts of this group spread knowledge of Western art and its techniques so widely throughout the Japanese art world that artists such as Hokusai and Hiroshige, whom the West viewed as standard-bearers of Japanese tradition, were already quite "Westernized" in their way.)

Thus, Japan was known to the Western world long before it "reopened" in the mid-nineteenth century. That knowledge was of course fragmentary and sometimes embellished with fantasy, but it was widespread. For example, the 1726 book *Gulliver's Travels*—whose author, Jonathan Swift, was Dean of St. Patrick's Cathedral in Dublin, Ireland, and probably never even visited continental Europe, let alone Japan—describes an audience with the "Emperor of Japan" in Edo with great accuracy (although, of course, the audience should have been with the shogun rather than the emperor). Swift was evidently familiar with German physician Engelbert Kaempfer's account of his years in Japan, published in 1712. Kaempfer visited Japan as a Dutch ship's physician and was present at two audiences with the shogun, in 1691 and 1692. His *History of Japan* was published posthumously in 1727, first in English, but quickly translated into other languages, making a great contribution to Europe's knowledge of Japan. It was followed by numerous other records of travels in Japan and disquisitions on the country published before the mid-nineteenth century. Among the most important were the accounts of voyages by Carl Peter Thunberg (in Japan 1788–1793), Adam Johann von Krusenstern (1810–1812), and Hendrik Doeff (1833). Isaac Titsingh also published five books on Japan between 1819 and 1834, and the renowned Philipp Franz von Siebold wrote extensively on the country starting in the 1830s, after living there from 1823 to 1828.

This interest in Japan was reflected in the European art world, with traces visible as early as the seventeenth century. For example, painter Nicolas Poussin's *Miracle of St. Francis Xavier* (1641–1642) depicts Xavier bringing a girl back from the dead in Kagoshima, while Jacques Callot made a copperplate engraving entitled *The Martyrs of Japan* (ca. 1627) showing the infamous mass crucifixion of 1597. However, although each work takes an episode from the Christian missionary project in Japan as its subject, the connection is purely thematic. The style is not Japanese in the slightest.

Even so, Japanese art, and particularly Japanese craftwork, was already gathering strong acclaim across Europe. Many tiny gold and silver *maki-e* cabinets created for export to the Iberian Peninsula survive, and royal collections contain *maki-e* bureaus, shelves, chests, and other items of furniture from the period. Western enthusiasts quickly acknowledged the skill and refinement of Japanese artisans in creating lacquerware of this kind.

Among English speakers, the word "japan" came to mean lacquerware in much the same way that "china" came to mean porcelain. John Stalker's *Treatise of Japanning and Varnishing* was published in 1688,[3] and the term remained in wide currency throughout the eighteenth century. In the first edition of the *Encyclopedia Britannica*, published 1771, the entry for "Japan" is just three lines long—but the entry for "japanning" devotes over two hundred lines to a detailed description of what it calls "the art of varnishing and drawing figures, &c. in the manner as is done by the natives of Japan."

Similarly, Japanese ceramic wares were welcomed alongside those from China by connoisseurs across Europe. When political turmoil on the Asian mainland made it impossible for the Dutch East India Company to purchase Chinese porcelain between 1658 and 1729, vast quantities of Arita ware from Japan were brought to Europe instead, playing a significant role in the birth of Dresden porcelain.[4] Thus, by the end of the eighteenth century, the West was home not only to considerable knowledge of Japan but also to countless examples of actual Japanese crafts (even if they were often confused with *chinoiserie*).

But what about painting? A dearth of surviving artwork and documentary evidence makes it difficult to say anything definite, but promising leads do exist. Edmond de Goncourt's celebrated book *Hokousaï*, published in 1891, claims that Hokusai painted two picture-scrolls for the manager of the Dutch trading house, who wished to take them back to Europe as souvenirs. According to Goncourt, "the first depicted all the stages of life for a Japanese man, from birth to death, and the second all the stages of life for a Japanese woman." What is more, Goncourt said, Hokusai made copies of these scrolls for the ship's doctor as well, and "continued to sell a number of sketches to the Dutch" afterward.[5] Stories of this sort should not be uncritically accepted, but this case does carry a certain weight because it was discussed in Japan as well prior to Hokusai's death in 1849.[6] The fate of those four scrolls bound for Holland, and indeed the later sketches Hokusai sold the Dutch— assuming they really existed—remains unknown. Still, we cannot exclude the possibility that Hokusai was known to the West much earlier than is usually believed.

An even more promising topic for our investigation is the collection of Isaac Titsingh, who headed the Dutch trading house in Nagasaki on three occasions between 1779 and 1784 and was a great admirer of Japanese art. The collection's existence has been confirmed, and according to several sources, including a (partial) catalog published in Amsterdam in 1893,[7] it contained craftworks such as ceramics, ornaments, and *netsuke*, along with scrolls of paintings, color prints, and richly illustrated books. Titsingh, who died in 1812, spent most of his final decade in Paris,[8] so it is not hard to imagine that some of the city's residents noticed his collection. However softly, the wind from Japan had already begun to blow in Paris.

Jean-Auguste-Dominique Ingres is one nineteenth-century painter who must be reconsidered in this historical context. Consider the following oft-cited passage from *L'atelier d'Ingres*, a memoir published by Ingres's pupil Amaury-Duval in 1878 at the height of *japonisme*:

> The Japanese paintings that a young and novel school believe they have discovered were admired by M. Ingres more than sixty years ago; the proof is in his *Portrait of Madame Rivière* and the Pourtalès *Odalisque* [currently in the Louvre's collection as *Grande odalisque*], of which the critics said, "This work resembles the colored designs that sometimes adorn Arabic or Indian manuscripts."[9]

It is unfortunate that Amaury-Duval offers no further information about the Japanese art that Ingres "admired," but his tone is so firm and confident that it does seem likely he was writing based on specific knowledge. Although there is no proof that Ingres had seen any Japanese paintings, or even prints, his interest in Japan is evident in a passage from the ninth volume of his *Notes*, currently held by the Musée Ingres in Montauban. In the passage, he describes a plan to paint "several scenes from the life of a hero" inspired by "Japanese chronicles."[10] Overall, however, there is not enough evidence to affirm or deny a Japanese influence on Ingres. For now, the question must remain open.

But if that is so, what *should* we make of the similarities between a certain kind of work by Ingres and the art of Japan? The omission of as much modeling as possible, the arrangement of bright, unshadowed colors, the lack of depth, the proclivity for curved lines, the close attention to lucid detail—do we not detect these many idiosyncrasies of Ingres's style in the work of Kōrin and Utamaro as well? On a purely superficial level, would it not be better to call Ingres "a *Japanese* painter lost in the ruins of Athens"?[11]

The truth is that these qualities of Ingres's art, dismissed by critics of his age as "primitive," were born of his ceaseless quest for perfection and new forms of expression. Accordingly, even if he was familiar with Japanese art—which, I repeat, has not been proven—we could hardly call this the primary factor in his innovations. This "rebellious disciple of David," as Théophile Silvestre described him, might not have realized it himself, but he was one of the first exponents of the innovative modern movement that prioritized painting over illusion and style over reality. Although Ingres himself did not reject re-creation of the visible world as an artistic principle, that movement would, by the end of the nineteenth century, finally arrive at Maurice Denis's celebrated "flat surface covered with colors assembled in a certain order."[12]

Thus, in Ingres's case, any commonality with Japanese artists reveals less a relationship of influence than an encounter, an interaction—and a necessary rather than coincidental one, at that. As we will see, the role of Japanese art as a kind of catalyst only becomes more pronounced in the latter half of the nineteenth century. This explains why *japonisme* was so thriving and important at that time.

— 3 —

When Japan "opened" itself to the outside world following the appearance of Commodore Perry and his US naval fleet off Uraga in 1853, everything changed. Trade, travel, and expositions carried great quantities of Japanese craftwork, prints, writing, and other goods to the West, launching the true "age of *japonisme*." By the 1860s, zeal for Japan was widespread. Even Jean-François Millet and Théodore Rousseau, two painters who lived in seclusion in the French village of Barbizon, became so competitive about collecting Japanese prints that they almost had a falling out. However, while many sources and testimonials affirm their interest in Japan, it is difficult to find convincing signs of influence in their paintings—curiously, the exact opposite of the situation with Ingres.

For example, the anecdote about Millet and Rousseau's quarrel is conveyed to us by Alfred Sansier,[13] and an 1864 letter from Millet offers additional support. Neither painter's work, however, displays the clear "Japanese" characteristics seen in Ingres's. Still, many art historians have attempted to find traces of Japanese influence there, and several have even concocted hypotheses about specific paintings by Millet. The most noteworthy is probably the suggestion by Kobayashi Taichirō that the pose of the nude in Millet's 1863 painting *The Goose Girl* (Walters Art Museum, Baltimore) derives from one of Utamaro's famous *Abalone Divers* (*Awabi-tori*) triptychs.[14] This is an incisive observation, but we must consult many other types of sources before accepting it as truth. I expect that further traces of *japonisme* may await discovery in Millet's late works in particular—his pastels, for example, with their Utamaro-esque atmosphere (as noted by Geneviève Lacambre), and his unusual nightscapes.

Sansier also claims that, before Rousseau submitted *Le village de Becquigny* to the Salon in 1864, he repainted the entire sky, "giving it a sapphire-colored glow like a Japanese sky." As a result, Sansier says, the picture "attained a glow by means of bold colors like those employed in the Japanese prints that so fascinated him at the time."[15] However, as Rousseau died just three years later, his subsequent artistic career was insufficient to fully develop whatever he had found in those prints.

In the subsequent age of Manet and the Impressionists, the craze for all things Japanese spread like wildfire and burned for nearly half a century.

This period has been addressed from many perspectives already, particularly over the past quarter of a century. I will avoid discussing individual artists here, and instead restrict myself to two more general observations. The first is about the artistic side of the phenomenon, and the second about the wider social and cultural context.

The mania for Japanese art began as an interest in rare and exquisite things, but rapidly transcended mere exoticism to become closely intertwined with the revolutionary activities of those now called the "avant-garde." Unlike the Orientalism favored by Academic artists like Gérôme and Gleyre, *japonisme* was popular with independent painters searching for new forms of expression outside the Salon system. These artists were determined to break free of traditions of illusory re-creation of reality that had been in place since the Renaissance. The art of Japan offered a solution to their dilemma in "the unexpectedness of its compositions, the science of its forms, the richness of its colors, the originality of its pictorial effects, and . . . the simplicity of the means employed," as critic Ernest Chesneau put it in the passage from *La Japon à Paris* cited in Chapter 6.[16]

In other words, it was not the *oiran* in sumptuous clothing or landscapes with Mount Fuji in the background that were of interest, but the actual forms of expression: compositional novelty, exquisite lines, bold colors, and simplified technique. This was precisely the new aesthetic about to change the face of Western art.

Painters did not succumb haplessly to the temptation of Japanese art—at least, not the most talented among them, like Manet, Whistler, Degas, and Monet. Even as they raved over the mysterious beauty of ukiyo-e, each one, in their way, acquired new methods for even greater self-expression. Japanese art was not simply an outside model to be followed unquestioningly. It was also an important catalyst allowing these painters to express what was within them more clearly. Chesneau, a superb critic, understood this well. In the essay cited above, he describes what these painters found in Japanese art as "not just inspiration, but confirmation of their individual ways of seeing, feeling, understanding, and interpreting nature."[17]

Artists understood this as well as Chesneau. After visiting an exhibition of prints by Hiroshige and Utamaro at the Durand-Ruel Galleries organized by the art dealer Samuel Siegfried Bing (who usually simply went by "S. Bing"), Pissarro wrote a letter to his son Lucian on February 3, 1893, reading, "the Japan exhibition was stupendous. Hiroshige is a wonderful Impressionist painter. . . . These Japanese artists *confirm* that our way of thinking is not mistaken" (emphasis added).[18]

There is no doubt that the innovative movements of the avant-garde of the time were particularly convenient and fertile soil for Japanese influence. The extent of any influence, not to mention the fruit it bears, depends not just on its own power but also on the readiness of its recipient. Nothing can bear fruit unless the recipient is prepared for its arrival. Even in the first half of the nineteenth century, Japanese art was not entirely unknown in the West. But as long as the aesthetic of faithful reproduction achieved through perspective and shading retained authority, Japan was nothing but another foreign country. Not until Western aesthetics as a whole began to falter did Japanese art became so powerfully influential.[19] This explains the wide appeal of *japonisme* in the second half of the nineteenth century—and its near disappearance after 1900, except in the fields of architecture and ornamentation, even as Japanese art became better known than ever.

My second observation pertains not to art itself but to the special nature of art in Japan as an inextricable part of daily life. Almost all early Western visitors to the country emphasized this point: in Japan's cultural traditions, art is not a separate world isolated from quotidian existence but a completely natural part of life. The idea of the artwork as an independent, self-ordered microcosmos, so important in the West, was entirely absent from Japanese thought. Even practical, everyday items had a constant tendency to become art, while artworks in the more conventional sense had a constant role to play in an everyday life that was itself extremely artistic. This is why the finest works of art in Japan are invariably displayed at particular times and places to which they are appropriate, like the scrolls hung in tokonoma alcoves for specific gatherings. This custom was upheld even at the 1900 Exposition universelle in Paris, where visitors were irked to find that some of the scrolls at Japan's pavilion were only displayed for a limited time. The tradition survives even in modern museums, an institutional model imported from the West: folding screens depicting plum blossoms or irises, for example, are often displayed only when those flowers are in bloom. Obviously, this is done partly in a spirit of conservation, to ensure that especially fragile artworks are safely preserved, but the psychological foundations supporting the tradition go much deeper. When Van Gogh says that, in Japan, "the drawings, the curiosities, are hidden in drawers" (Letter 509, Van Gogh Museum translation), we can only admire his perspicacity.

In other words, this is a matter of national culture. In fact, starting with the 1876 Exposition universelle—the first one in which Japan officially participated—the Japanese pavilion at every World's Fair has displayed art within scenes of everyday life. Put another way, scenes of daily life are surrounded by art. Entire dwellings and farmhouses were re-created at exposition venues for the purpose of displaying artwork inside, with tea sometimes offered to visitors in the traditional manner by young, female attendants. S. Bing, an art lover and dealer blessed with deep insight, fully understood how crucial this fusion of art and daily life was in Japan when he founded the lavish art magazine *Le Japon artistique* in 1888. As the magazine's title clearly indicates, his goal was to introduce Western readers not simply to "Japanese art," but to "artistic Japan"—the country as a whole.[20]

Bing may have been one of the more knowledgeable visitors to the Japanese pavilion at these expositions, but the wordless message emanating from the Japanese artwork appears to have been understood to some degree by a broader audience. One reporter who visited the 1878 exposition wrote:

> As for the tastes of this race [i.e., the Japanese], what their art has revealed to us is confirmed in other areas: they are practical above all, drawn to what is useful, but to those useful forms they add spontaneously, as if by intuition, the finery of an imagination that is ingenious, playful, rich in surprises and good humor.[21]

It seems to me that this reevaluation of the applied arts, of the fortuitous combination of practicality and beauty, was exactly the ideal promoted by the various fin-de-siècle movements now grouped under terms like "Art Nouveau" and "Jugendstil"—including the English Arts and Crafts movement and the Free Aesthetics of Brussels—that concerned themselves with art's artisanal side. I do not mean to imply that *japonisme* was the sole cause of this revolution in design, of course. Still, the idea of art as a unified whole, so strongly advocated by votaries of these new aesthetics, had already been realized with a high degree of refinement in Japan. And, in fact, European artists and critics of the age often eagerly brought Japanese art into their arguments. For example, in his 1891 essay "On the Role and Influence of the Arts of the Far East and of Japan," Roger Marx says:

> The influence of the Far East stands clearly manifest as an accomplished fact. They who henceforth would forget it would condemn themselves to ignore in part the origins of modern evolution . . . and to fail to discern what constitutes, though we do not know it, the style of to-day. In thus doing they would be ignoring in the history of the variations of art the instance of an all-powerful influence, with which only the influence of antique art on the age of the Renaissance can be compared on equal terms.[22]

These words, coming as they do from a critic who was deeply conversant in history, are further evidence of how large Japan loomed in the minds of people of that age. And so we can finally be satisfied that what took place was an encounter between two cultures, an exchange of ideas in the truest sense— and one of a most fertile and productive nature.

Notes

1. Michel Melot, "Questions du Japonisme," in *Japonisme in Art: An International Symposium*, ed. Society for the Study of Japonisme (Tokyo: Committee for the Year 2001 and Kodansha International, 1980), 245.

2. Geneviève Lacambre, "Les milieux japonisants à Paris, 1860–1880," in *Japonisme in Art*, 43.

3. Yamada Chisaburō, "Shinoazuri kara japonezuri e," in *Japonisumu no jidai: Jūkyū seiki kōhan no Nihon to Furansu*, ed. Dainikai Nihon Kenkyū Nichifutsu Kaigi (Tokyo: Nichifutsu Bijutsu Gakkai, 1983), 5. Dr. Yamada was an important supporter of this exhibition.

4. Yamada Chisaburō, "Shinoazuri kara japonezuri e," 7.

5. Edmond de Goncourt, *Hokousaï* (1904: repr., Paris: Union Générale d'Editions, 1986), 147–48.

6. This episode appears in volume 31 of *Koga bikō* as "Tenpō jūnen rokugatsu tōka shin'i-bō no hanashi" (Conversation with a Certain Acupuncturist on Tenpō 10.6.10). In Asaoka Okisada, *Zōtei koga bikō*, vol. 2 (1904; repr. Tokyo: Shibunkaku, 1970), 1408–1409.

7. *L'art japonais: Collection du Dr J. Titsingh à La Haye, contenant 775 numéros, don't 384 objets céramiques, les autres netzkés, statuettes, bronzes, laques et livres* (Amsterdam: Frederik Muller & Cⁱᵉ, 1893). Kobayashi Taichirō, "Ōshū geijutsu ni okeru Nihon eikyō no tansho" (1938–1939), in *Kobayashi Taichirō chosakushū*, vol. 2 (Kyoto: Tankōsha, 1974), 272. Part of Titsingh's collection, including paintings, prints, and drawings, was reportedly already in the possession of the publisher A. Nepveu in 1818 (Kobayashi, "Ōshu geijutsu," 241–243).

8. Kōda Shigetomo, "Isaaku Tichingu" (1938), in *Kōda Shigetomo chosakushū*, vol. 4 (Tokyo: Chūō Kōronsha, 1972), 197–217.

9. Amaury-Duval, *L'Atelier d'Ingres* (Paris: G. Charpentier, 1878), 281–282. See also the discussion by Daniel Ternois of *Madame Rivière* and *Grande odalisque* in the catalogue of the Ingres exhibition held at the Petit Palais in Paris, *Ingres* (Paris: Petit Palais, 1967–1978), 28, 102–104.

10. Geneviève Lacambre, "Japonisme," in *Petit Larousse de la Peinture*, vol. 1, ed. Michel Laclotte (Paris: Larousse, 1979), 917.

11. These are the slightly altered words of Théophile Silvestre, referring to Jean-Auguste-Dominique Ingres. The original quotation is *"un peintre chinois égaré en plein XIXe siècle, dans les ruines d' Athènes"* ("a Chinese painter lost in the nineteenth century in the ruins of Athens"). Théophile Silvestre, *Les artistes français*, vol. II (Paris: G. Charpentier, 1926), 37.

12. Maurice Denis, "Définition du Néo-traditionnisme" (1890), in *Théories (1890–1910)* (Paris: Bibliothèque de l'Occident, 1912), 1.

13. Alfred Sensier, *La vie et l'œuvre de J. F. Millet* (Paris: A. Quantin, 1881), 258–259.

14. Kobayashi Taichirō, "Ōshū geijutsu," 264–266.

15. Prosper Dorbec, *L'Art du paysage en France* (Paris: H. Laurens, 1925), 127. According to materials in the Louvre's Cabinet des dessins, after the end of the Salon exhibition, Rousseau altered *The Village of Becquigny* again, returning the sky to its original color. Cf. the information for 1864 in Marie-Thérèse de Forges, "Biographie," in Musée du Louvre, *Théodore Rousseau (1812–1867)*, catalogue of an exhibition held at the Musée du Louvre in 1968, and Bernice Davidson, *The Frick Collection: An Illustrated Catalogue*, vol. 2 (New York: The Frick Collection, 1968), 180.

16. Ernest Chesneau, "La Japon à Paris," *Gazette des Beaux-Arts*, September 1878, 387.

17. Ernest Chesneau, "La Japon à Paris," 396.

18. Camille Pissarro, *Lettres à son fils Lucien* (Paris: Albin Michel, 1950), 298.

19. In a book about Monet's "Water Lilies" paintings at the Musée de l'Orangerie, Michel Hoog notes that as early as Louis Vitet's review of the 1826 Salon exhibition, there were mentions of "Japanese screens and chests" and "flat fields of color." Says Hoog: "the two-dimensional representational arts of Japan . . . were known in the West long before 1850, but they were seen as belonging to a mode of representation that was completely foreign to Western art, and so were rejected as models." Michel Hoog, *The Nymphéas of Claude Monet at the Musée de l'Orangerie*, trans. Jean-Marie Clarke (Paris: Réunion des Musées Nationaux, 1987), 65.

20. Cf. Ôshima Seiji, *Japonisme* (Tokyo: Bijutsu Kōronsha, 1980), 218 and after.

21. Édouard de Beaumont, et. al., and Louis Gonse (ed.), *Exposition universelle de 1878: Les Beaux-Arts et les Arts Décoratifs* (Paris: Gazette des beaux-arts, 1879). Quoted in *Le Livre des Expositions Universelles, 1851–1989* (Paris: Union Centrale des Arts Décoratifs, 1983), 73.

22. Roger Marx, "On the Role and Influence of the Arts of the Far East and of Japan," *Artistic Japan*, vol. VI, 1891, 459.

Part III

PASSING BEAUTY, RETURNING MEMORY

11. The Aesthetics of Transition
The Four Seasons and the Japanese Sense of Beauty

— 1 —

Among the holdings of the Suntory Museum of Art in Roppongi is a pair of four-panel folding screens known as *Birds and Flowers in Autumn and Winter* (*Shūtō kachō-zu*). Painted in rich colors on a field of gold, the work was actually created in the sixteenth century as a single screen, eight panels wide. At the far right of the composition is a pine tree surrounded by early autumn flora, including Japanese bush clover, Chinese bellflowers, and valerian. To the left of this, at the center of the painting, is a more deeply autumnal pine beside a maple with crimson leaves, while on the far left is a pine covered in pure white snow set among other evergreens such as the fern pine and *hinoki* cypress. The scenery depicted ranges from autumn to winter—or, put another way, the season changes slowly from autumn to winter as we look across the image from right to left. The original eight-panel screen was itself the left side of a pair; the screen on the right depicted spring and summer, so that the entire sixteen-panel set depicted a full cycle of the four seasons.

Shiki-e or "four-season paintings" like this were produced in great number and variety in the late Muromachi and particularly the Edo period. Even within the medium of folding screens, many examples come to mind: Sesshū's *Birds and Flowers in Four Seasons* (*Shiki kachō-zu*, Kyoto National Museum), Kanō Motonobu's work of the same name (Hakutsuru Fine Art Museum), Kaihō Yūshō's *Landscapes in Four Seasons* (*Shiki sansui-zu*, MOA Museum of Art), Geiai's *Birds and Flowers of the Four Seasons* (*Shiki kachō-zu*,

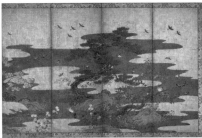

Anonymous, *Birds and Flowers in Autumn and Winter* (*Shūtō kachō-zu byōbu*). Suntory Museum of Art.

Kanō Tan'yū, *Pines of the Four Seasons* (*Shiki matsu-zu byōbu*). Daitokuji temple. Image: Kyoto National Museum

Kyoto National Museum), and, in the late Edo period, Matsumura Keibun's *Flowering Plants of the Four Seasons* (*Shiki sōka-zu*, Okura Museum of Art) and Ikeda Koson's *Stream and Flowering Plants of the Four Seasons* (*Shiki sōka ryūsui-zu*). Each of these depicts scenery and natural phenomena for each of the four seasons in turn. Flowering plants and birds are rendered in such vivid color and fine detail that the screens could almost serve as horticultural or ornithological references if the subjects were treated in isolation instead of gathered together to form seasonal tableaux.

Like the first set of screens mentioned, in each of these works the seasons change from right to left across the same image. The paintings depict scenes from nature, but also changes within nature—that is, the passage of time itself. In a work like Kanō Tan'yū's *Pines of the Four Seasons* (*Shiki matsu-zu*, Daitokuji temple), the use of the evergreen pine as a motif strengthens the impression of time passing around it. This is a major feature of Japanese painting not found in Western art from the same period.

Many Western painters produced depictions of the four seasons, of course.

Jean-François Millet, *Spring (Daphnis and Chloë) (Le Printemps (Daphnis et Chloé))*. National Museum of Western Art. The Matsukata Collection. Photo: NMWA / DNPartcom

Nicolas Poussin's *Four Seasons* series (*Quatre saisons*, Musée du Louvre) is one well-known example in the French Classical tradition. Celebrated eighteenth-century court painter François Boucher also painted a pastoral set of the same title (Frick Collection). In all of these works, however, each season was assigned its own individual painting. Poussin's *Four Seasons* combines each season with a scene from the Bible—"Spring (The Earthly Paradise)," "Summer (Ruth and Boaz)"— representing each like a still photograph. According to customs dating from the Renaissance, tableau paintings of this type depicted an independent and unchanging world: fixed, unmoving physical and temporal perspective was a fundamental principle. This tradition was handed down unchanged until the nineteenth century.

Jean-François Millet, a painter of the Barbizon school, completed three *Four Seasons* sets in his life, each comprising four individual works. *Spring (Daphnis and Chloë)*, in the collection of Japan's National Museum of Western Art, is from one of those sets, having originally adorned the walls of financial tycoon Charles Xavier Thomas's residence in Paris. Of its fellows, *Summer (Ceres)* is now owned by the Musée des Beaux-Arts de Bordeaux, *Winter (Cupid, Frozen with Cold)* by the Yamanashi Prefectural Museum of Art, and *Autumn* was destroyed in a fire. The *Spring* from Millet's later years, in the collection of the Musée d'Orsay, was also part of a four-piece set whose other members are currently in Boston, New York, and Cardiff.

Each of these paintings was an individual, independent world, within which perspective and time were unchanging.

The situation did not change even with the arrival of the Impressionists, who were exquisitely sensitive to changes in nature's form not only in relation to the seasons but also under different climatic conditions and at various times of day. Monet is known for his particularly strong interest in light, and painted outstanding sets of paintings featuring subjects like haystacks or the Rouen Cathedral in morning, noon, and evening light. Nevertheless, each work captures its subject in the light of a single moment. To paint not just these momentary appearances but the aspect of light itself as it changed, he would have had to remove the edges delineating each individual work and connect them into a single great painting. Indeed, the *Water Lilies* murals he painted in his final years, now at the Musée de l'Orangerie (see p. 59), were done in just this way: they depict the changing appearance of the lily pond from early morning to late evening in a single uninterrupted work, like a gigantic picture-scroll. In the context of Western art history, this was a highly idiosyncratic approach, and Monet himself admitted that his deep affection for and sympathy with Japanese art lay in the background of the project.

To return to Japan, *shiki-e* were found not only on folding screens but in many other formats, including hanging scrolls, sliding room partitions, and picture-scrolls. Hanging scrolls conceived as part of four-scroll sets tend to be relatively independent from each other. On the other hand, paintings on partitions were designed to form a single uninterrupted image (*fusuma-e*) when the partitions were fully shut; examples include Kanō Eitoku's *Flowers and Birds of the Four Seasons* (*Shiki kachō-zu fusuma*) for Daitokuji Jukōin temple, and Kanō Mitsunobu's *Flowers and Trees of the Four Seasons* (*Shiki kaboku-zu*) at Onjōji Kangakuin temple.

In picture-scrolls, the continuity of the image is even more obvious. Picture-scrolls were not designed to be viewed all at once, as they sometimes are in books and museums today. Instead, they were to be unrolled only enough to see a certain length of the image as the viewer scrolled

Kanō Mitsunobu, *Flowers and Trees of the Four Seasons* (*Shiki kaboku-zu fusuma*). Onjōji Kangakuin temple.

through them from beginning to end. The effect is an image that slowly changes before the viewer's eyes. The convenience of this arrangement for depicting the passage of time made the picture-scroll a popular format for tales and narratives, but they were also used to depict natural scenes that changed with the seasons. Few would deny that Sesshū's *Landscapes of the Four Seasons* (*Shiki sansui-zu*, Mohri Museum) is the most distinguished example of this.

So suited to Japanese aesthetic sensibilities was this approach of depicting multiple seasons in a single continuous image that artists continued producing such works into the twentieth century, including Hishida Shunsō's *Landscape of the Four Seasons* (*Shiki sansui*, National Museum of Modern Art, Tokyo) and Yokoyama Taikan's work of similar name (*Shiji sansui*, Yokoyama Taikan Memorial Hall).

Sesshū, *Landscapes of the Four Seasons* (*Shiki sansui-zu maki*) (detail). Mohri Museum.

— 2 —

One particularly intriguing example of *shiki-e* is Sakai Hōitsu's *Flowering Plants of Summer and Autumn* (*Natsu-aki kusa-zu*, Tokyo National Museum) set of folding screens (see pp. iv-v). Currently preserved as a pair of free standing two-panel screens, the work was painted on the back of Ogata Kōrin's *Wind God and Thunder God* (*Fūjin raijin-zu*, Tokyo National Museum)—which is itself a copy of Tawaraya Sōtatsu's work of the same name at Kenninji temple. The work thus connects three generations of masters of the Rinpa school. Whether Hōitsu had Sōtatsu's painting in mind as he worked is unknown, but he had the deepest respect for Kōrin, and *Flowering Plants* is unmistakably both a response and homage to the older painter's *Wind God and Thunder God*. What is intriguing is that, in painting this direct homage, Hōitsu chose a completely different subject.

The Wind God and Thunder God arrived in Japan from the continent. The image of the Thunder God with a ring of drums on his back seems to be a Chinese invention, but the roots of the other deity and his sack of winds originate much farther away, in the so-called "Western Regions" (roughly corresponding to today's "Central Asia"), and may even be traceable as far as the eastern Mediterranean. In any case, the two gods met in China. The earliest known artwork depicting both is a ceiling mural in Mogao Cave 249, Dunhuang, dated to the beginning of the sixth century. The deities arrived in Japan along with Buddhism, and were depicted in many forms. Some-

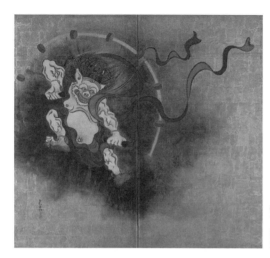

Ogata Kōrin, *Wind God and Thunder God (Fūjin raijin-zu byōbu)* (detail). Tokyo National Museum. Image: TNM Image Archives

times they were servants appearing with Kannon and her retinue, as in the Seikado Bunko Art Museum's *Thousand-Armed Kannon and Twenty-Eight Attendants*; at other times, they were sculpted individually, as seen in the Sanjūsangendō hall in Kyoto.

Sōtatsu and Kōrin's paintings of the two figures are iconographic inheritors of this tradition—allegorical personifications of nature, symbolic of its power, rather than beings supposed to actually exist. Hōitsu, however, transmutes these celestial deities into concrete, natural earthly forms. One of his screens shows a river, swollen by an evening shower, flowing behind miscanthus, morning glories, and lilies in the rain; the other depicts kudzu leaves in typhoon winds, including some already being carried away. These scenes are rich in seasonality, the first of summer and the second of autumn. That Hōitsu meant this as a response to Kōrin's painting is clear from a note in his own hand pasted on the back of a study for the screens, very nearly at scale, in the collection of the Idemitsu Museum of Arts. "Thunder God—summer flora, rain," reads the note. "Wind God—autumn flora, wind." With this, Hōitsu seizes celestial deities transcending time itself and drags them down to Earth to become everyday natural scenery connected to the progression of the seasons.

Frontispiece, "Parable of the Medicinal Herbs" (*Yakusōyu-hon*), Kunoji Sutras (*Kunōji-kyō*). Private collection. Image: Nara National Museum, Photograph © Sasaki Kyosuke

Tamamushi Satoko's superb book *Flowering Grasses of Summer and Autumn: Silver Remembrance* (*Natsu-aki kusa-zu byōbu: Tsuioku no gin'iro*)[1] provides more details regarding the historical pedigree and meaning of Hōitsu's work, and I have relied on her work to inform much of this essay. As it happens, she introduces another compelling example of coded seasonal representation.

At the end of the Heian period, faith in the Lotus Sutra was widespread, and the practice of copying the sutra out was at its zenith. Among the surviving copies, the Kunōji Sutras (preserved at Tesshūji temple and elsewhere) include a certain frontispiece to the "Parable of the Medicinal Herbs" chapter. The illustration depicts two nobles standing with umbrellas in the gentle rain and gazing at the vibrant green foliage around them. This is a pictorial representation of the chapter's text, which compares the universal compassion of the Buddha to the rain that falls on all plants indiscriminately. But the picture does not show just any rainfall. It is based on a specific poem that Fujiwara no Shunzei wrote about a verse from the Lotus Sutra at the request of Taikenmon'in (the name adopted by Fujiwara no Tamako, empress consort of Emperor Toba, when she became a nun at the end of her life). The poem reads as follows:

Kanō Osanobu. *Agriculture in the Four Seasons (Shiki kōsaku-zu byōbu)*. Suntory Museum of Art.

harusame wa	spring rains
kono mo kano mo no	falling hither and yon
kusa mo ki mo	on flowering plants
wakazu midori ni	and trees, have
shimuru narikeri	dyed them green

In the sutra, rain is a simple metaphor, with no particular season specified. Shunzei narrows this down to the "spring rains" that revive the foliage. That this frontispiece is a reference to Shunzei's poem is revealed by hints in the picture itself: the three birds in the sky, and—somewhat inappropriately for the season—a case of luggage by a nobles' umbrella. These were part of a popular rebus-like code: three birds (*mi tori*) and luggage (*ni*), combine to form *midori ni* ("green"), quoting enough of Shunzei's well-known poem to confirm that this picture also depicts the rains of spring.

— 3 —

Another key characteristic of *shiki-e* is that they often portray nature as deeply linked to human activity. This includes depictions of mundane tasks

like farm work, in which the rhythms of everyday living unfold alongside nature (or, rather, in accordance with it); annual occasions for enjoying and admiring the changes of nature, like blossom- and moon-viewing; and the various festivals that are closely connected to the kinds of work and play enjoyed in each season.

One of the most direct instances of this is the "Agriculture in the Four Seasons" genre, which was highly popular in the early modern period. As the name suggests, these works depict the labor done on farms over the course of a year, from sowing seeds in spring through transplanting rice seedlings and weeding in summer to harvesting and husking in autumn, all amid seasonally changing natural scenery. Well-known examples include paintings by Kusumi Morikage (Kyoto National Museum) and Iwasa Matabē (Idemitsu Museum of Arts). Yosa Buson, a master of Nanga painting, also produced work in this genre, although all examples are now in private hands. All of the works mentioned above are pairs of six-panel folding screens, depicting the progression of time from right to left as usual (except Morikage's, which go from left to right).

As a concrete example, consider Kanō Osanobu's *Agriculture in the Four Seasons* (*Shiki kōsaku-zu*, Suntory Museum), painted during the Bunsei era

(1818–1830). The rightmost part of the right-hand screen depicts mountains covered in the wild cherry blossoms of spring. At the foot of the mountains, people till the fields beneath cherry trees in full bloom. Continuing left, we see people transplanting seedlings, waterways in summer, and then autumn scenes on the right edge of the left-hand screen. This is followed by people busily bringing in the harvest, and finally, on the far left, mountains capped with snow. The entire year is deftly shown as a continuous unit.

But one year is not the end. People knew well that when winter passed, spring would be back again. In the Suntory Museum's *Birds and Flowers of Autumn and Winter*, discussed earlier, bush warblers (*uguisu*) perch on the snow-covered boughs of the pine at the far left. Bush warblers are considered harbingers of spring, and their appearance in a winter scene anticipates the coming thaw. It is an allusion to the fact that seasons do not just change but repeat in a cycle. Nature follows its endless circuit around and around, for all eternity, and humans live their lives in step with its progress.

Annual observances tied to particular seasons rather than the seasonal cycle in general play a large role in Japanese life, and were often taken up as subjects by painters. Masterpieces like Kanō Naganobu's *Merry-Making Under Aronia Blossoms* (*Kaka yūraku-zu*, Tokyo National Museum), Kanō Naizen's *Festivals of Toyokuni* (*Hōkoku sairei-zu*, Toyokuni Shrine), and Kanō Hideyori's *Maple Viewers* (*Kanpū-zu*, Tokyo National Museum) all fit this description. These works are normally treated as genre paintings, but their connection to the relevant season is significant and nature is usually a powerful presence throughout the painting as a whole. Some even found ways to bring in the seasonal cycle as a whole after all. For example, the main focus of *Maple Viewers* is the crowd of people admiring the crimson autumn foliage and conversing over packed meals, but the sight of Mount Atago's snowy peak at the far left hints at the coming winter. Customs and tradition were dependent on the flow of the seasons, too.

Nor was this deep connection between the seasons and human life restricted to the nobility. It was strongly rooted among everyday folk as well, as can be seen in Hiroshige's *One Hundred Famous Views of Edo* (*Meisho*

Kanō Hideyori, *Maple Viewers on Mount Takao (Takao kanpū-zu byōbu)* (detail). Tokyo National Museum. Source: ColBase (https://colbase.nich.go.jp/)

Edo hyakkei) ukiyo-e series from the late Edo period. After publishing five of these prints in the second month of 1856, including "Blossoms on the Tama River Embankment" (*Tamagawa-zutsumi no hana*) and "Ohashi Bridge at Senju" (*Senjū no ōhashi*), Hiroshige continued to work on individual "famous views" from around the metropolis. He produced 37 over the rest of the year, 71 in 1857, and 10 more in 1858, for a total of 118 before his death. His publisher added one more work by Hiroshige II (the original Hiroshige's disciple and son-in-law) plus a "Contents" page (frontispiece) by Baisotei Gengyo and published the set of 120 illustrations to great acclaim. The prints were divided into four seasonal sections. Hiroshige may not have intended this division, but the prints themselves do have an undeniable seasonal feel, from "Plum Estate, Kameido" (*Kameido umeyashiki*) and "Maple Trees at Mama, Tekona Shrine and Linked Bridge" (*Mama no momiji Tekona no yashiro tsugihashi*) to "Snow on Bikunihashi Bridge" (*Bikunihashi Setchū*). In this respect, the seasonal categorization emerges of its own accord. The Edoites, after all, enjoyed each "famous view" (*meisho*) in the appropriate season.

The word *meisho*, corresponding to "famous view(s)" in the translated title above, literally means "famous place." It originally referred simply to places that people enjoyed visiting, and seasonal features were important factors in this popularity. Mount Yoshino was famed for its cherry blossoms

Utagawa Hiroshige, "Fine Weather After Snow on Nihonbashi Bridge" (*Nihonbashi yukihare*), *One Hundred Famous Views of Edo* (*Meisho Edo hyakkei*). Tokyo National Museum. Source: ColBase (https://colbase.nich.go.jp/)

in full bloom and the Tatsuta River for its brocade of autumn foliage. Even in Edo, a metropolis of one million, that tradition survived unchanged.

What's more, as famous as these sites may have been, they were still part of everyday life, used for everything from blossom- and moon-viewing to festivals and observances. This is reflected in Hiroshige's collection: The spring section begins with "Fine Weather After Snow on Nihonbashi Bridge" (*Nihonbashi yukihare*), in which Mount Fuji looms in the background above Nihonbashi bustling with the first shipment of the new year, followed by "Kasumigaseki" (*Kasumigaseki*) where children are flying kites and playing battledore and shuttlecock. "Suidobashi Bridge and Surugadai" (*Suidōbashi Surugadai*) is a close-up of a carp streamer for the Children's Festival in the fifth month, while "Sumiyoshi Festival at Tsukudajima" (*Tsukudashima Sumiyoshi no matsuri*) depicts the summer festival at Sumiyoshi Myōjin Shrine. In more than a few cases, the observances are the primary subject of the work, such as in "Flourishing City, Tanabata Festival" (*Shichū han'ei tanabata matsuri*) and "Ryogoku Fireworks" (*Ryōgoku no hanabi*). In Hiroshige's work as in the general understanding of the phrase, "famous views" combined places, seasons, and everyday life.

— **4** —

This resonance with the cycle of the seasons finds expression not only in fine art but also in literature and theater. Short-form poetry like tanka and haiku is an obvious example. In the *Kokin wakashū* or *Kokinshū* (Collection of old and current Japanese poems) of 905, the first imperially commissioned anthology of Japanese poetry, the works are not arranged by author as they would be in a Western or Chinese anthology. Instead, they are arranged according to the flow of the seasons, from spring to winter. The flow of seasons was viewed as more important than authorship.

This seasonal division was preserved in the next imperial anthology, the *Shin kokin wakashū* (New collection of old and current Japanese poems), followed by many others over the generations. Indeed, it became the basic format for Japanese anthologies. Fujiwara no Kintō's *Wakan rōeishū* (Collection of Japanese and Chinese poems for singing), which was completed not long after the *Kokin wakashū* and served as an anthology of outstanding poetic models in Chinese and Japanese for centuries to come, also adopted a seasonal arrangement. It began with *risshun*—the first solar term of spring in the traditional East Asian calendar.

In haiku, connections to the seasons are even more evident, including the formal requirement of including a *kigo* or "seasonal word." So far as I know, this has no parallel in any other poetic tradition. Many, but not all, *kigo* refer directly to natural phenomena like "cherry blossoms" or "snow." Other *kigo* are related to human activity, like *koromogae* (changing one's wardrobe for the new season) and *susuharai* (literally "brushing away the soot," but equivalent to "spring cleaning" in English). Despite the efforts of some haiku poets in the Meiji period and after to promote "seasonless haiku," a great many Japanese people still enjoy composing seasonal haiku in the traditional form, relying on the profusion of published books known as *saijiki* ("chronicles of the year") that list seasonal words and associations. If anything, changing lifestyles have only increased the stock of seasonal words. One *saijiki* I happen to have on my desk lists some 2,500 *kigo*, a number that might seem unimaginable to those unfamiliar with Japanese culture.

Even outside the realms of tanka and haiku, attention to and appreciation for the rich beauty of the changing seasons finds expression in many forms across Japan's literary tradition and way of life. The opening of the *Pillow Book*, written in the late tenth century, is one celebrated example:

> In spring, the dawn; the mountains brighten at the edges, growing paler as thin wisps of purple cloud drift across the sky . . .

These lines are as vivid as any wash drawing in their depiction of natural serenity in the fresh atmosphere of an early spring morning. Author Sei Shōnagon continues season by season, identifying the most moving time of day: in summer, the night; in autumn, the evening; in winter, the early morning. Appreciation for the beauty of change is a common thread throughout.

Just as the seasons repeat their procession with each year, the cycle of day and night begins anew with every morning. Time moves in endless, unceasing circles, and nature's form evolves with it. Neither the fresh beauty of a spring dawn nor the poignant landscape of an autumn evening lasts for long. The ever-changing form of nature nurtured within the Japanese soul the idea that beauty is transient, fleeting, and for that reason all the more precious. In the West, examples like the beauty of bodily proportions show the existence since ancient Greece of a strongly held belief that beauty arises when certain standards are satisfied, and is to that extent eternal and unchanging. In Japan, however, beauty was understood to fade with the passage of time. This made feelings of tenderness for things soon to be lost an important element in aesthetic consciousness.

For example, one of the *kigo* used in haiku is *yuku haru*, "passing spring." This refers to the time when spring is nearing its end and summer is approaching, but it evokes more than this description may suggest. For a Japanese reader, the phrase contains within it poignant regret *for* the passing of spring. This is exactly why Bashō includes it in the haiku closing the scene in *Narrow Road to the Deep North* where he bids farewell to his close friends before departing on his long journey:

> *yuku haru ya*   departing spring—
> *tori naki uo no*   the birds cry, the fish
> *me wa namida*   are teary-eyed

No one can stop the cycle of the seasons, and no mortal can avoid partings. Bashō imagines the very birds and fish sharing his sadness on the occasion, layered with the wistfulness of passing spring.

A similar example from the realm of painting is Takeuchi Seihō's *Regret for the Passing of Spring* (*Sekishun*, 1933). Most of this work is taken up by a carelessly stacked pile of bundled firewood. Before this, in the foreground, lies scattered firewood yet to be bundled. In terms of genre, it is a still life of a commonplace subject—perhaps a rural yard that Seihō painted from life. Atop the pile of firewood perches a bush warbler, associated with the coming of spring, and the image is scattered with pale pink cherry blossom petals. In practical terms, this signals that the time of blossoming is nearing its end. Symbolically, the contrast of rough firewood and delicate flower petals—they look as if they might dissolve at the touch—practically cries out to the viewer with its message that fleeting, transient things are beautiful and to be cherished because of that fragility. It is a remarkable expression of the emotions evoked by the idea of "passing spring." We might also cite Kawai Gyokudō's *Passing Spring* (*Yuku haru*, 1916), a landscape showing a stream in a rocky valley entirely filled with dancing flower petals, or Ikeda Yōson's *Recalling Spring* (*Sekishun*, 1980), which shows the petals scattered instead across the surface of a body of water in which is reflected a five-storied pagoda—a superb visual representation of the Japanese soul.

To see a world of beauty in petals even as they scatter and fall is a uniquely Japanese sentiment, nurtured by the cycle of seasons. Flowers in full bloom are a feast for the eyes, of course, and gladden the heart. But falling flowers have their own poignant appeal. Similarly, while moon-viewing remains popular in Japan, it is not restricted to admiration of the full moon

Takeuchi Seihō, *Regret for the Passing of Spring (Sekishun)*. Nakanoshima Museum of Art, Osaka.

high in the sky. Lists of haiku *kigo* include not only *jūgoya* ("fifteenth night"—the night of the full moon in a traditional lunar calendar), but many other moon-related words and phrases: *jūsanya* ("thirteenth night"), *izayoi* ("sixteenth night"), *tachimachizuki* ("standing and waiting for the moon" to come out). The *Pillow Book* has much praise for moonlight—"In summer, the night; still more when the moon is full"—but Sei Shōnagon was also moved by the beauty of the fireflies on moonless nights, and found rainy nights to have their own appeal. Kenkō Hōshi reveals the same aesthetic consciousness in *Essays in Idleness* (*Tsurezuregusa*) when he asks rhetorically, "Are flowers to be viewed only when in bloom, and the moon only when perfectly full?"

In traditional Western aesthetics, beauty has defined standards. To fail to meet those standards is to be imperfect and therefore of lesser value. The Japanese, however, saw what might be called the beauty of the imperfect. Intimately familiar with ever-changing nature, they lived in close accord with the flow of time, and amid its many transitions—of which the four seasons are just one example—they cultivated a rich and varied realm of beauty.

Note
1. Tamamushi Satoko, *Natsu-aki kusa-zu byōbu: Tsuioku no gin'iro* (Tokyo: Heibonsha, 1994).

12. "The Color of the Flowers"
Symphonies of Image and Word

In his book on Surrealist painter René Magritte, French philosopher Michel Foucault writes:

> Two principles, I believe, ruled Western painting from the fifteenth to the twentieth century. The first asserts the separation between plastic representation (which implies resemblance) and linguistic reference (which excludes it). . . . The two systems can neither merge nor intersect.[1]

Put simply, images and words belonged to utterly separate worlds. Indeed, in the tableau pictures that constituted the mainstream of Western art from the Renaissance onward, the painted image is expected to cover the entire canvas, with the painter's almost apologetic signature in the corner as the only text. There is certainly no room for sentences or paragraphs.

Japan, however, has countless examples of words and images coexisting, on folding screens, sliding room partitions, picture-scrolls, hanging scrolls, and other media. In the "poem-and-painting scrolls" (*shigajiku*) of the Muromachi period, blank space was left above the image to be filled with poetic commentary and appraisal, creating a duet of picture and text. Adorning a screen painting with poems it inspired was a customary event at celebrations in the Heian period. For example, the "Poems of Celebration" section of the *Kokinshū* contains the following work by Ki no Tsurayuki:

haru kureba	when spring comes
yado ni mazu saku	the first to flower in my yard

ume no hana	are the blossoms of the plum
kimi ga chitose no	which seem to me a garland
kazashi to zo miru	for your thousand years, my lord

The explanatory text before the poem states that it was "written on the rear folding screen at Prince Motoyasu's seventieth birthday celebration." In other words, the venue had a folding screen with a merry picture of plum blossoms painted on it, to which Tsurayuki added his elegantly calligraphed poem. Many other *byōbu-uta*, or "folding screen poems," have been preserved, but the screens themselves have all been lost. As a result, we do not know whether the poems were written directly onto the screens or on a separate piece of paper that was then pasted on, but the result is the same either way: painting, poetry, and calligraphy coexisted in a single work of art, mutually resonating to the delight of viewers.

Similar traditions from over the centuries have survived in Japan to this day: anthologies of poetry hand-copied onto lavishly ornamented paper, the Rinpa school's works combining calligraphy and illustration on square pieces of card (*shikishi*) or in scroll format (*utamaki*), and even the cards used to play *karuta* in everyday households on New Year's Day, which feature both poems and images. The relationship between word and image was extremely free and diverse. At times, the text was written right on top of the picture, as seen in fan-shaped Lotus Sutras or Tawaraya Sōtatsu and Hon'ami Kōetsu's *Crane Scroll* (*Tsuru shita-e waka-kan*). Words and images were not separate worlds. They merged and gave birth to a rich new creative realm.

When Foucault spoke of the separation between plastic representation (pictures) and linguistic representation (words), the tectonic shifts caused by the printing technology developed during the Renaissance were surely in the forefront of his mind. Printing made it easy to produce books in bulk, but illustrated books had to be printed in two passes using two completely different methods: movable type for the text, and—usually—copperplate printing for the illustrations. To ensure that this went smoothly, word and image had to be kept clearly separate in the page layout. The two elements had never truly merged in the West, not even in medieval illuminated manuscripts, but printing technology made their separation decisive.

In Japan, things were different. By the Edo period, Japan was a "kingdom of print" with few peers in the world, but woodblock printing was the norm in almost every genre and format: art books, illustrated tales for popular consumption like *kibyōshi*, and even ukiyo-e. Although multicolored printing required multiple blocks, woodblock printing made it easy to carve image and text into the same block and combine them freely. *Kibyōshi* like Master Flashgold's Splendiferous Dream (*Kinkin-sensei eiga no yume*), in which every inch of free space was crammed full of text, were only possible because printers were using woodblocks.

The Japanese were not unfamiliar with Western printing technology. In the Azuchi-Momoyama period, movable type introduced by Christian missionaries enjoyed great if temporary popularity, and wooden typefaces were cut and used to publish a great many "old movable type books" (*kokatsuji-bon*), as they are now known. The early seventeenth-century "Saga-bon" books, published by Suminokura Ryōi with the help of calligrapher Hon'ami Kōetsu in the village of Saga near Kyoto, are well-known examples. At roughly the same time, Tokugawa Ieyasu, who was passionate about collecting and disseminating books, also had a series of "Suruga-ban" books printed in Suruga province (modern Shizuoka prefecture) and elsewhere, using metal type that survives to this day. However, movable type failed to gain real traction, and was gradually forgotten as woodblock printing grew ever more dominant. Movable type simply could not compete with woodblocks as a way to include pictures and text as equals on the same page.

In the West, since medieval times, paintings were created with brushes while text was written with quill pens, and later metal-tipped pens. Thus, pictures and words were distinguished even by the tools used to produce them. In Japan, however, the same brush was used for both pictures and text. Across the entire East Asian cultural sphere, centered on China, calligraphy and painting were viewed as fellows, as can be seen from the existence of compound words like *shoga*, "calligraphy and painting." This was, above all, due to the nature of the writing system.

The letters of the English alphabet are pure phonograms. Their shapes carry no meaning whatsoever. On the other hand, Chinese characters are both phonograms and ideograms, highly figurative in nature. The character for "mountain" (山) is shaped like a mountain, and the character for "river" (川) derives from representations of flowing water. Japan uses not only Chinese characters (known in Japanese as kanji) but also two phonemic syllabaries created in Japan, hiragana and katakana (known collectively as kana). The expressive power of this writing system is highly multifaceted, allowing many combinations of pictures and text to enrich the world of Japanese art.

As early as the Heian period, the court nobility enjoyed an elegant game in which the flowing curves of hiragana were used to depict riverside scenes— or, one might say, the characters were hidden within the scenes. This game, called *ashide-e*, is described in detail in the *Tale of Genji*. In the Edo period, the age of mass culture, this taste for concerts of word and image spread among the common folk. *Moji-e* ("character pictures") and *emoji* ("picture characters") flowered to popular delight. There were *henohenomoji* faces and *hemamusho nyūdō* (human figures drawn with kana and sometimes kanji); *hanji-e* (pictures challenging the viewer to decipher the words they represented); and pictorial calendars combining artistic expression with utility. Santō Kyōden's *Kimyō zui* (Bizarre illustrated dictionary) was a book of pictorial word games; Hokusai's *Ryakuga haya-shinan* (Quick guide to sketching) was a textbook on *moji-e*. The enormous popularity of these works and others like them shows the public hunger for such entertainments.

The *Six Poetic Immortals* (*Rokkasen*) series, also by Hokusai, is a masterpiece of word–image combination. Consider his drawing of Kisen Hōshi ("Kisen the Priest"). The top of the page contains Kisen's poem in *Hyakunin isshu* (One hundred poems from one hundred poets), its characters artfully scattered in the technique known as *chirashigaki*:

> *waga io wa*   my little hut
> *miyako no tatsumi*   is southeast of the capital

Left: Katsushika Hokusai, "Kisen Hōshi" (Kisen the Priest), *Six Poetic Immortals* (*Rokkasen*). Rivoli Antiques.
Right: The characters hidden in the image.

shika zo sumu	and so I dwell
yo o ujiyama to	amid the hills of Uji
hito wa iu nari	woeful, so they say

Below that is a portrait of Kisen in his priest's robe, the folds of which conceal the hiragana characters in his name. It is a consummate accomplishment.

As an example of the *ashide-e* technique repurposed, consider the stunning "Hatsune" *Maki-e* Box (*Hatsune maki-e tebako*) in the collection of the Tokyo National Museum. This was made for the trousseau of Chiyohime, daughter of the the third Tokugawa shogun Iemitsu, and is ornamented to an accordingly lavish degree. As the name suggests, the principal technique used was *maki-e*—intricate images executed in gold powder within the lacquer. The box's lid bears an image based on the "Hatsune" chapter of *The Tale of Genji*, in which the Lady of Akashi sends a poem to her daughter,

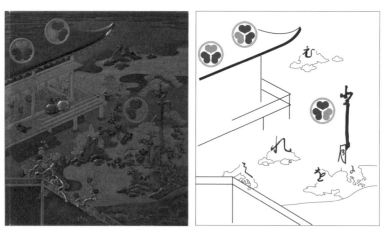

Left: "Hatsune" *Maki-e* Box (*Hatsune maki-e tebako*). Tokyo National Museum.
Source: ColBase (https://colbase.nich.go.jp/)
Right: The characters hidden in the image.

currently in the capital with Genji, to express her feelings as she waits for correspondence from her:

toshitsuki o	let she who has waited
matsu ni hikarete	months and years, drawn
furu hito ni	always to the pine
kyō uguisu no	hear this day the warbler's
hatsune kikaseyo	first spring song

The image depicts part of Genji's mansion, the Rokujōin, and its garden. A single warbler is perched on the railing, and an old pine stands in the garden. On close examination, the pine's branches form the character *to*, its trunk is an elongated *shi*, its roots form the kanji read *tsuki*, and the character *o* is off to one side. *To – shi – tsuki – o*: the first line of Akashi's poem. The rest of the poem can be found hidden elsewhere in the picture. This confirms that the picture is not just of any mansion, but Genji's in particular, which is why the piece is specifically called the "Hatsune" *Maki-e* Box.

Note that, although the pine tree is drawn with hiragana and kanji, it

Pontoon Bridge *Maki-e* Writing Box (*Funabashi maki-e suzuribako*). Tokyo National Museum. Source: ColBase (https://colbase.nich.go.jp/)

also stands in for the word *matsu*, which means both "pine" and "wait." In letters and text messages between today's young people, it is not uncommon for a letter or word to be replaced by a picture, and these *emoji* were also used by playful Japanese literati. For example, the haiku poet and painter Yosa Buson, in a letter of thanks enclosed along with an umbrella he was returning to a friend, used a picture of the umbrella to stand in for the word "umbrella."

The Pontoon Bridge *Maki-e* Writing Box (*Funabashi maki-e suzuribako*), also in the collection of the Tokyo National Museum, is another craftwork expertly decorated with a *chirashigaki* poem that incorporates *emoji*. Made by the calligrapher Kōetsu, its lid has a bold, dramatic design with boats in relatively high relief and a band of lead placed across them that stands in for the bridge. Scattered across the entire surface is a poem by Minamoto no Hitoshi from the *Gosen wakashū* (Later selection of Japanese poetry):

azumaji no	like the pontoon bridge
Sano no funahashi	of Sano in the east
kakete nomi	my longing spans
omoiwataru o	the space between us
shiru hito zo naki	known to none

The finished product is superbly expressive, brimming with poetic sentiment. At a glance, it seems to be missing the word *funahashi*, "pontoon bridge," but this is because the image itself represents the bridge.

The unrestrained, even capricious placement of the characters is also worth noting. They are scattered about with utter freedom. The first three lines, minus the word *funahashi*, are written on the central bridge. The text then jumps up to the top section and continues: *omoiwataru / shiru hito no.* Finally, the bottom section finishes the poem with *naki.* A person who did not know the original verse would not even know where to begin reading. Kōetsu evidently believed that the poem was widely enough known that this would not be a problem. The same can be said of the "Hatsune" *Maki-e* Box. There was a certain cultural climate in which creator and viewer shared knowledge of classical literature, and in the Edo period this kind of classical education reached even the common folk.

If familiarity with the classics could be assumed among viewers, then there was no need to write out the entire text of a quoted poem. A single line—a hint, effectively—should be sufficient to reveal the meaning, and more in the spirit of the Japanese aesthetic of "conveying the whole by a fragment." This is the case in another priceless lacquerware item, the Hare's Foot Fern *Maki-e* Writing Box (*Shinobu maki-e suzuribako*). The box's cover is entirely covered with fern designs, and written over these are five characters in lead plate that read *tare yue ni*, roughly "for whom." From these words alone, the viewer was expected to easily recall the poem by Kawara no Sadaijin (Minamoto no Tōru) in the *Kokinshū*, later included in the *Hyakunin isshu*:

michinoku no	as, in the north,
shinobu mojizuri	with ferns they stain their cloth,
tare yue ni	for whom else
midaresomenishi	so roughly dyed would I
ware naranaku ni	have thus become?

The ferns behind the letters were, of course, also meant to help viewers recall the poem.

As this tendency toward abbreviation progressed, written characters were removed entirely so that allusions to poems were made through image alone. Ogata Kōrin's Yatsuhashi *Maki-e* and Mother-of-Pearl Writing Box (*Yatsuhashi maki-e raden suzuribako*), a National Treasure, is a fine example of this. This lacquer box is lavishly decorated on every side with irises and winding bridge motifs executed in mother-of-pearl. Its theme is the ninth chapter of the *Tales of Ise*, in which Ariwara no Narihira sees the irises blooming by Yatsuhashi (literally "Eight Bridges") in Mikawa Province on his way to the east. He responds by composing a poem in which each line starts with one character of the word *kakitsubata*, "irises":

ka*ragoromo*	familiar as
ki*tsutsu narenishi*	a robe long worn
tsu*ma shi areba*	is my wife, and having
ha*rubaru kinuru*	left her far behind
ta*bi o shi zo omou*	I brood on my journey

(Note that by the orthographic rules of the time, *ha* was equivalent to *ba*.)

The *Tales of Ise* were as well known as the *Tale of Genji*, and inspired many folding screens, picture-scrolls, and ukiyo-e. Normally, an illustrated version of this scene would depict it as described, with a picture of the melancholy Narihira contemplating the distant capital alongside his bitterly weeping retinue. However, Kōrin excises Narihira and his traveling companions, expressing the *Tales of Ise*'s lyrical worldview with nothing but flowers and bridges. The images on the writing box are a depiction of the text (poem), and in that sense must be "read" just as one would a book.

Kōrin also painted a folding screen based on the same classical reference: *Irises* (*Kakitsubata-zu*) (see p. 82), a National Treasure in the Nezu Museum collection. In this work, he eliminates even the bridge, creating a composition in which the vivid flowers are arrayed before a dazzling field of gold. In purely visual terms, the effect is breathtaking, but the realm of *Tales of Ise* unmistakably lies behind it. Kōrin's method of cutting away story elements one by one until only the core image of the flowers remains to signify everything else exemplifies the Japanese aesthetic of negation discussed in Chapter 1.

Pictures based on poems, or designed to evoke poems, were also called *uta-e* ("poem-pictures"). One such highly idiosyncratic *uta-e* is the Sano Ford *Maki-e* Writing Box (*Sano no watari maki-e suzuribako*) in the collection of the Gotoh Museum.

This box, also said to be the work of Kōrin, has no text inscribed on it. Nevertheless, it is known to be a pictorial representation of a poem by Fujiwara no Teika in the *Shin kokinshū*:

koma tomete	to stop their horse
sode uchiharau	and shake their sleeves
kage mo nashi	there is no one
Sano no watari no	before the Sano ford
yuki no yūgure	in evening snow

The connection is the picture on the box's cover of a noble on horseback shaking his sleeves high above his head. This imagery is certainly based on the poem, but we cannot call it a depiction of the text as such. Teika specifically describes a snowy evening *without* human figures. He begins the poem with two lines evoking a richly attired noble, then immediately negates them ("there is no one") to heighten the loneliness of the verse. This skillful use of rhetoric is itself an application of the "aesthetic of negation." Teika was a master of such devices.

Lyric poetry drawing parallels between human emotion and natural phenomena is not rare in the West. We might list the poetry of Pierre de Ronsard, which expressed his love of roses, or Goethe's *Song of Mignon*, full of longing for southern climes—in Thomas Caryle's translation:

> Know'st thou the land where citron-apples bloom,
> And oranges like gold in leafy gloom . . . ?

Then there is Paul Verlaine, who expressed his painful love for his beloved as "many fruits and flowers, leaves and branches." To translate these poems to the pictorial realm would not be difficult. One need only draw some flowers and fruits. But this is not the case for a poem like the following, also by Teika:

miwataseba	surveying the view
hana mo momiji mo	of flowers and autumn leaves
nakarikeri	there is no sign—
ura no tomaya no	a rush-thatched hut
aki no yūgure	by the bay in autumn dusk

How could a world like this be rendered pictorially? It begins with imagery of cherry blossoms (by Teika's time, the word *hana* (flowers) alone conveyed this meaning) and vivid autumnal imagery. But, again, this is immediately negated: "of flowers and autumn leaves / there is no sign." This kind of negative rhetorical technique can also be seen in Bashō's haiku:

kono michi ya	this road—
yuku hito nashi ni	walked by no one
aki no kure	on an autumn evening

or Shimazaki Tōson's lines:

midori nasu	green-growing
hakobe wa moezu	chickweed has not sprouted
wakakusa mo	the young grass
shiku ni yoshi nashi	covers not the ground

It is a Japanese aesthetic tradition linking poets and authors in a great chain.

The maker of the Sano Ford *Maki-e* Writing Box reversed this negation and actually drew the subject who is not supposed to be there. But this, too, is a kind of rhetorical device: as viewers, we first admire the courtier in his finery as an image, then recall Teika's poem and imagine the courtier's absence, leaving only a desolate, deserted snowbank. Though highly contrived, this is of rich artistic interest. The picture and the text—or to borrow Foucault's terminology, the plastic representation and the linguistic reference—are inseparably bound together in a masterful duet.

As noted above, the general population became familiar with the classics during the Edo period. Knowledge was transmitted through many media, from illustrated books and ukiyo-e to the theatrical stage. The popularity of the game of *karuta* illustrates this phenomenon. *Karuta*, which could be called the national New Year's Day pastime, is played using two decks of cards with poems from the *Hyakunin isshu* on them. One deck has cards with the full text of a poem and a picture of the poet. These cards are called the *efuda* or *yomifuda*, "picture cards" or "reading cards" respectively. The cards in the other deck bear only the second half of each poem. These are called the *jifuda* or *torifuda*, "text cards" or "taking cards." Someone not currently playing reads one of the *efuda* aloud, and the players race to be the first to find the corresponding *jifuda* on the floor. Even children unfamiliar with the poems can play a game called *bōzu-mekuri* ("priest-flipping"), where types of cards are distinguished solely by the type of poet depicted—nobleman, noblewoman, emperor, or priest. Even today, many Japanese no doubt fondly recall New Year's mornings spent playing this game. In *karuta*, word and image are one, resonating with each other to form an elegant artistic world.

A verse by Ono no Komachi offers a window onto the way these poems reverberated through popular culture:

hana no iro wa	the color of the flowers
utsurinikeri na	has faded and passed on
itazura ni	in vain
wa ga miyo ni furu	have I spent my life
nagame seshi ma ni	watching the long rains fall

"Ono no Komachi," *Hyakunin isshu*.
Saga Arashiyama Museum of Art and Culture.

The collection of Saga Arashiyama Museum of Arts and Culture has a stunning set of illustrated *karuta* that includes this poem. The *efuda* depicts a radiant Komachi alongside her name and the first half of the poem (in the earliest versions of the game, the *efuda* did not include the full poem). The *jifuda* contains only the poem's second half, but the calligraphy is so supple, so daring and expressive that it is a work of art in itself. In another *karuta* set, the so-called "Kōrin *Hyakunin Isshu*," the *jifuda* also includes a painting by Kōrin of wildly blooming cherry blossoms. *Efuda* and *jifuda* together make up a dazzling world of ornamentation.

The *Hyakunin Isshu* was so well known that its poems even inspired parodies called *kaeuta*. Some of the *kaeuta* became popular in their own right. For example, the *Edo meisho hyakunin isshu* (Famous views of Edo *Hyakunin isshu*), published during the Kyōhō era (1716–1736), contains this poem alongside Komachi's name:

hana no koro wa	cherry blossom season
sakarinikeri na	has reached its peak
Uenoyama	on Ueno Hill
wa ga mi bentō o	have I opened
aki seshi ma ni	my *bentō* boxed lunch

This is paired with an illustration of people enjoying a feast within a curtained-off area as they admire the Ueno cherry trees in full bloom. The puckish Edoites loved poetic parodies of this nature. Another one, from the *Gosen ikyokushū* (Later selection of rustic poems), based on the same poem goes:

hana no saki wa	the tip of my nose
sogarenikeri na	has been removed
itazura ni	in vain
wa ga maotoko to	with my paramour
nagane seshi ma ni	did I oversleep

This exploits the fact that *hana* can mean either "flower" or "nose" in Japanese, and refers to the punishment of partial rhinotomy for adultery. *Kaeuta* have no entertainment value unless the listener knows the original poem, so knowledge of Komachi's poem was clearly widespread among the populace.

Even stranger is Hokusai's take on the poem in his book *Hyakunin isshu uba ga etoki* (Nanny's illustrated explanations of the *Hyakunin isshu*). This is a work of what might be called pictorial parodies, completely recontextualizing the original poems. For Komachi's poem, the scene is moved to a mountain village in cherry blossom season, where women are busily taking advantage of the temporary bursts of sunshine between the "long rains" of spring to wash and dry their laundry.

Meiji-era artists like Kajita Hanko and Aoki Shigeru also produced paintings based on the *Hyakunin isshu*. It is worth noting that even contemporary artists often include the text of a poem alongside their pictorial representation of it.

In duets of word and image like this, the text is often written in very diverse ways, particularly in comparison with Western calligraphy. Dark and light shades of ink are used, thick lines and thin, large shapes and small, with characters freely arranged within the image. The expressive effect of this is more than evident in the examples raised so far, but another highly regarded work is the *Crane Scroll* (*Tsuru-zu shitae wakakan*). This was a col-

Hon'ami Kōetsu and Tawaraya Sōtatsu, *Crane Scroll* (*Tsuru-zu shitae wakakan*) (detail). Tokyo National Museum. Source: ColBase (https://colbase.nich.go.jp/)

laboration between calligrapher Hon'ami Kōetsu and painter Tawaraya Sōtatsu, and incorporates a poem traditionally attributed to Kakinomoto no Hitomaro:

honobono to	dimly, faintly
Akashi no ura no	off Akashi Bay
asagiri ni	in the mists
shimagakure yuku	slipping away behind the islands
fune o shi zo omou	the boat in my thoughts

The characters of the text are freely scattered about the image, sometimes using *hentaigana* (alternate forms of kana no longer in common use). Their visual call-and-response with the lithe cranes of the painting has a highly refined effect. In this work, the text serves not just the "function of reference"; it also plays the role of a plastic representation.

This approach was not seen in the West, even before the age of printing. When writing out a poem, consistency of letterform and line placement was a basic requirement. One rare counterexample is Mallarmé's *Un Coup de dés jamais n'abolira le hasard* (A throw of the dice will never abolish chance), published in 1897. This book uses free layouts and typefaces of different sizes to create a kind of alphabetic *chirashigaki*. At the time of the book's publication, it was viewed as a highly avant-garde experiment. The Japanese influence is clearly visible: Mallarmé was strongly interested in Japanese art, and seems to have been specifically inspired in this case by a book called *Poèmes de la libellule* (Poems of the dragonfly). This lavishly presented anthology of Japanese poems, translated into French, was published in 1885 by the poet Judith Gautier with the assistance of her friends Saionji Kinmochi, future Prime Minister of Japan, and painter Yamamoto Hōsui. As well as pages with the original poems written in *chirashigaki* calligraphy by Hōsui, the anthology includes at least one full page for each poem's translation. Over a Japanese-style background illustration of, for example, dragonflies or bats in flight, three textual elements are printed: a romanized version of the original poem, a French translation, and the name of the poet. Different typefaces are used for each element, and the elements are scattered across the page in a form of *chirashigaki*. Sometimes the text is superimposed directly on the background images, a design choice which must have felt refreshing to Western readers.

On the subject of the coexistence of word and image, it is also worth recalling that when Van Gogh, a passionate fan of Japanese art, made a copy in oils of "Plum Estate, Kameido" (*Kameido umeyashiki*) from Hiroshige's *One Hundred Famous Views of Edo*, he painted Japanese characters in the left and right margins (see p. 121). Hiroshige's original ukiyo-e does not include this text, which has nothing at all to do with the image. Presumably, Van Gogh simply added some characters he had seen in a different ukiyo-e, thinking this the height of Japaneseness.

As a final example of the masterful combination of word and image, I would like to mention the work of internationally renowned twentieth-century printmaker Munakata Shikō. Munakata's *Wandering Away from Home* (*Ryūrishō*) series contains pictorialized versions of poems by his friend Yoshii Isamu, and his *Poems by Tanizaki Jun'ichiro* (*Utauta hanga-saku*) series uses lines from the famous author, who was a friend of Munakata's.

Munakata Shikō, "Sumiya" (*Sumiya no saku*),
Wandering Away from Home (*Ryūrishō hanga-saku*).
Ohara Museum of Art.

These prints combine text and illustration in bold new ways, lavishly conveying the profound sentiment of the poems as well as Munakata's startling creative abilities. The thousand-year tradition in Japanese art of combining images and words remains well and truly alive.

Note

1. Michel Foucault, *This Is Not a Pipe*, 2nd ed., trans. James Harkness (Berkeley, University of California Press: 2008).

13. The Heritage of Memory
Intangible Culture as Japanese Tradition

What Is Authenticity?

In 1993, Himeji Castle and Hōryūji temple became the first Japanese cultural assets to be added to the UNESCO World Heritage List, attracting a great deal of commentary. The following year, seventeen temples and shrines in Kyoto, Uji, and Otsu—including the Phoenix Hall at Byōdōin, which strongly influenced Frank Lloyd Wright—were jointly added to the list as the "Historic Monuments of Ancient Kyoto." The year after that saw the addition of the "Historic Villages of Shirakawa-gō and Gokayama."

The World Heritage List is based on the goal of protecting priceless cultural and natural heritage for future generations, in accordance with the World Heritage Convention adopted by UNESCO in 1972. When I originally wrote this essay in 1996, the list included 469 sites around the world, from the Great Wall of China to the Pyramid Fields of Egypt; today, it includes over a thousand. Japan ratified the convention in 1992, and this opportunity to share knowledge of the country's outstanding cultural assets widely around the world, rather than among a limited circle of specialists and intelligentsia, is an outcome to be celebrated. At the same time, it forces us to consider anew some questions about the very essence of Japanese culture. For, when Hōryūji was proposed as one of Japan's first entries on the World Heritage List, a serious debate arose among international committee members over how appropriate it would be to list Hōryūji at all.

One of the key requirements for a cultural asset to be inscribed on the World Heritage List is "authenticity." Assets that are not "authentic" are not considered worthy of inclusion—no fakes allowed, in other words. UNESCO recognizes several kinds of authenticity: authenticity of "location and setting," for example, and of "traditions, techniques and management systems." In the case of Hōryūji, doubts were raised about the authenticity of its "materials and substance"—specifically, about whether the materials in the building's structure were the original materials used when it was first built.

In Japanese wooden architecture, replacing damaged parts with new ones is a common conservation method. In the most extreme cases, the entire structure is rebuilt, as happens periodically with the Ise Grand Shrine. (The Ise Grand Shrine is not rebuilt simply for the purposes of conservation, of course, but the rebuilding does have a conservationist effect.) Perhaps because the regular rebuilding at Ise is so well known, when Hōryūji was presented for discussion, a committee member from the West reportedly inquired whether it was not the case that *all* of Japan's temples and shrines were rebuilt every twenty years.

This is a simple misunderstanding, of course. Hōryūji has not been rebuilt in this way. It is true, however, that over the course of its long history, the building materials in some parts have been replaced—which means that those parts are not "authentic" in that they do not contain the original materials. The question, I am informed, thus became what percentage of Hōryūji counted as authentic in this way.

In the end, Hōryūji was accepted for inclusion on the World Heritage List. Some of its materials are more recent, but the majority were deemed authentic. This is well and good for Hōryūji. But the Ise Grand Shrine is regularly rebuilt with new materials. Can we really call it "inauthentic"? As discussed in an earlier chapter, few if any Japanese people would agree with that assessment.

In the essay "Bunka bōeiron" (Defense of culture), Mishima Yukio identifies the idea that "the copy is the original" as one of the unique characteristics of Japanese culture, offering—yes—the Ise Grand Shrine as an example. Mishima also notes the same quality in Japan's emperor system, stating that "every emperor in the imperial line was in himself the emperor; the relationship between Amaterasu and the emperor is not one of original and copy."

Emperor system aside, it seems fair to say that the seemingly inconsistent idea of the Ise Grand Shrine being simultaneously copy *and* original is well established. But how can this be possible?

Born of Fragility: Inheritance of Form

The Pyramids of Egypt and the Parthenon of Greece are both what we call *monuments*. Monuments of various types have been built in the West and elsewhere, but all are rooted in a powerful desire to convey to untold ages the memory of a certain person or event. The very word *monument* derives from the Latin *moneo*, "to remind." Etymologically, a monument is a reminder.

The desire to keep memories of important events or people alive among later generations is a natural human urge. But human memory is unreliable and fragile; with the passing of time, remembrance is forgotten. A monument is an attempt to circumvent this by embodying remembrance in a more durable form. You might call it an attempt to guarantee the inheritance of memory within the durability of the material. (It is precisely because accumulation and inheritance of memory give culture form that monuments of this sort become "cultural assets.") If this is so, then authenticity of materials is indeed of decisive importance for monuments. If the original materials decay, the guarantee of memory's inheritance is broken. Given the strong orientation toward monuments in the West, it is only natural that authenticity of materials should be carefully weighed when determining cultural heritage status.

In Japan, too, the desire to ensure the eternal continuance of memory has been strong since antiquity. But the ancient Japanese did not erect monuments for that purpose like those in the West, because of an important insight: notwithstanding the failings and frailties of human memory, material things, too, eventually perish. Accordingly, instead of trusting in the durability of stone, they invented new methods for ensuring the inheritance of memory in a world where physical form is fleeting. These methods shared three key elements: inheritance of form, repetition of ritual, and connection to place. They can all be seen at work at the Ise Grand Shrine, but because of their surpassing Japaneseness, they are also evident in other cultural domains.

Let us consider inheritance of form first. The Japanese put no faith in the eternity of material objects, but they did believe form could endure forever. We cannot be sure that even the smallest details of the Ise Grand Shrine have remained unchanged over 1,300 years of rebuilding—in fact, it would be more reasonable to assume that some parts *have* changed. Indeed, old photographs show that the main shrine building (*shōden*) and two treasure halls (*hōden*) were located differently before 1889 than they are today. Notwithstanding these details, however, the important thing is the *idea* that the form has survived just as it was in ancient times. The purpose of rearranging those buildings during the 1889 construction was not to effect change but to return the shrine to (what was believed to be) its older, original form. Faith in the perpetuity of form assures the inheritance of memory.

Indeed, in Japan, unperishing forms do endure. This is why the history of architecture or painting in Japan does not fit the Western model, in which each new style takes the place of its predecessor. When the Gothic arrives, the Romanesque fades away. The Baroque replaces the Renaissance. When new interest in the Gothic style arose in the nineteenth century, it was not called a "continuation" of the original style but instead the "Gothic revival." History is a series of replacements and revivals.

This was not the case in Japan. The new architectural styles of the Kamakura period did not extinguish those of the Heian period, and when Western architecture arrived in the Meiji period, it took its place alongside those existing styles. The same is true of painting. The new does not replace the old; it is *added* to it, and the old survives as well—not in objects, but in forms.

Verbal expression—literature—also plays an important role in the inheritance of memory. In every country, literature is a key bearer of culture. Here, too, forms from ancient Japan have lived on and become cultural traditions. The *Kojiki*, a chronicle of Japan's most ancient historical period, contains poems in the 5-7-5-7-7 poetic form that has survived more or less continually to the present day—about as long as the Ise Grand Shrine, in fact. When the new 5-7-5 haiku form arose in the early modern period, it did not take the older form's place but flourished alongside it. Inheritance of form was also valued in classical performing arts like noh and kabuki, as well as in the tea ceremony and ikebana, indicating the widespread faith the Japanese place in form's perpetuity.

Repetition of Ritual

The second way of assuring eternal remembrance is repetition of ritual. The Ise Grand Shrine's value as the authentic, original shrine does not derive simply from the fact that it has the same shape as its predecessors. Just as important are the variety of rituals and observances performed according to unchanging custom since ancient times to ensure the reconstructed shrine's validity. The most central of these are the rituals of *sengyo* (transferring the object of worship in which the deity is thought to dwell to the newly constructed building) and *ōmike* (making the first offering of sacred foods in the new shrine, the day after *sengyo*), but there are many others performed during the process. The *yamaguchi-sai* propitiates the kami at the entrance to the sacred forest (*misoma-yama*) from which materials for the new building will be taken and offers prayers for the safety of those felling and transporting the timber. The *misoma-hajime-sai* is performed when the felling of the timber formally begins. The *okibiki-hajime-shiki* and *okibiki-gyōji* rituals are performed when the felled timber begins to be transported and arrives at the new construction site, respectively. During construction, the *chinchi-sai* pacifies the deities of the site; the *ricchū-sai* and *jōtō-sai* accompany the ritual of raising the pillars and ridgepole, respectively, of the *shōden*; the *nokit-suke-sai* is performed when thatching of the *shōden's* roof begins; and the *shin-no-mihashira-hōken* marks the placement of a symbolic post beneath the *shōden* at its center. Even counting only the most important rituals and observances, there are over thirty in all. For the 1993 rebuilding, the *yamaguchi-sai* was held on May 2, 1985—eight years before the new shrine was completed—and various preparatory steps began even earlier.

The rebuilding of the shrine is thus not solely a matter of construction, but also requires the completion of this multi-year chain of sacred rituals and observances. Those rituals adhere to forms transmitted from antiquity—and if we cannot be certain that they are exactly as they were thirteen hundred years ago, again, what is important is the intention to inherit the forms exactly as they were and the belief that this was done. For example, timber is not transported from mountain to work site by truck, but dragged there by human hands, as in times of old. According to Takano Kiyoshi's *Ise Jingū no nazo* (Riddles of Ise Grand Shrine), 173,000 people from all over Japan helped move the timber during the *okibiki-gyōji* in May 1986.[1]

In short, every time the Ise Grand Shrine is rebuilt, a process (believed to be) identical to the building process thirteen hundred years ago is followed. We might say that every twenty years, the shrine is reborn with new vital energy. This is why the Ise Grand Shrine survives, with each newly built incarnation both a copy made of new materials and an authentic original.

Linear Time and Circular Time

Even more important is the fact that these rituals, up to and including the actual reconstruction, take place over a set twenty-year period which endlessly repeats. (In reality, the schedule sometimes slips by a few years here and there for various reasons, and centuries passed during the war-torn medieval period with no rebuilding at all, but these are exceptions.) Repetition according to a set rhythm assures the inheritance of memory. Behind this principle lies the Japanese understanding of time as cyclical. Because it always returns to where it was before, it can be trusted to ensure that remembrance survives.

In contrast, in the West, time was seen as linear. It moved steadily away from its point of origin and brought oblivion and destruction. This is why "Father Time" is often depicted as an aged figure with a sickle, just like Death. "Thou nursest all and murder'st all that are," is the accusation leveled at Time in Shakespeare's *The Rape of Lucrece*.

The power of time to destroy was often described metaphorically as "the tooth of time." Art historian Erwin Panofsky offered many examples of this.

For example, in Shakespeare's *Measure for Measure*, Duke Vincentio says (act V, scene 1):

> O, your desert speaks loud; and I should wrong it,
> To lock it in the wards of covert bosom,
> When it deserves, with characters of brass,
> A forted residence 'gainst the tooth of time
> And razure of oblivion.

We might also consider François Perrier's seventeenth-century *Segmenta nobilium signorum et statuarum, quæ temporis dentem invidium evasere . . .* (Selection of the most celebrated statues to escape the envious tooth of time), with its frontispiece depicting a sickle-bearing Father Time literally gnawing on the Belvedere Torso. Time was a menacing agent of annihilation. To resist its ruthless work of destruction and oblivion and keep memories alive forever, monuments were built to last.

In Japan, however, time was more memory's friend than its destroyer. In time's repetitions, remembrance was reborn. This is why Japan has upheld so many rituals, festivals, and other annual observances connected to the cycle of time since antiquity. The West has yearly events, too, of course, as does the rest of the world. But just as the Japanese were particularly sensitive to the changes brought by the four seasons—even though those changes occur all around the world—so, too, did they place special importance on annual observances. Evidence of this can be seen, for example, in collections of haiku *kigo* (seasonal words), which include words for seasonal festivals and events alongside those for the natural characteristics of the season; or the large number of pictures depicting such observances in Hiroshige's *One Hundred Famous Views of Edo* (*Meisho Edo hyakkei*).

This is because both *kigo* and *meisho* ("famous views") are tied to human memory. A *kigo* is not just a symbol for expressing some aspect of the season, and a *meisho* is not just a place on the map. Since times of old, these words and places have been the bearers of countless memories, reflecting a vast inheritance of memory passed down in deeds repeated with every turning of the season. The power of memory stored in *kigo* is also a large part of why haiku, despite their brevity, can be so richly expressive.

There are countless examples of Japanese writers and artists taking up the four seasons as their subject, as the other essays in this book have shown. In the chapter "The Aesthetics of Transition," for example, we saw Fujiwara no Shunzei's "spring rain" poem as well as Sakai Hōitsu's *Flowering Plants of Summer and Autumn*, which reimagined Ogata Kōrin's *Wind God and Thunder God* in a remarkable "inheritance of form."

In the history of Japanese painting, genres like *shiki-e* (seasonal paintings) and *tsukinami-e* (paintings depicting activities performed in each of the twelve months of the year) arose early and were very popular. These works were simultaneously landscapes, often connected with *meisho* and annual observances, and genre paintings, but latent within all of them is the idea of time as an endlessly repeating cycle. As we have seen, when Western painters depicted the four seasons, they painted a separate image for each, while Japanese painters included multiple seasons in a single image. Nature remains in flux throughout the seasonal cycle, returning to its starting point with no discontinuity. This faith in the wheel of time ensured the inheritance of memory through cyclical repetition.

Connection to Place

The third key element in the inheritance of memory is connection to place. When the Ise Grand Shrine is rebuilt, the new shrine must be right beside the old one. The shrine cannot be built anywhere else. It is inseparably bound to the land it stands on, including the forest and the Isuzu River behind it. Since antiquity, the Japanese have believed that each place has its own special spiritual power, and that deepening their connections to those places allowed them to share in that power. Mountains and rivers were objects of awe and worship. Ōmiwa Shrine, thought to preserve the oldest type of shrine architecture in Japan, originally had only a worship hall, with no building for the kami to reside in—because that kami was Mount Miwa itself, at the foot of which the shrine stands. Similarly, at Kasuga Shrine, the sacred realm of the kami is the entire area known as Kasugano, including Mount Kasuga behind the shrine itself. In Western Christendom, the sacred space of the church and the secular space outside were clearly distinguished, but in Japan the power of place is always present.

Places with special spiritual power attracted visitors in large numbers. As these visitors prayed, offered praise, and composed songs and poetry, the places accumulated memories. *Utamakura*, specific places often mentioned in poetry, arose in exactly this way. If annual observances were moments in time at which memories accumulated, *utamakura* and *meisho* were points in space that worked the same way. Japanese culture developed by placing importance on these points in time and space. Just like the changing seasons, the natural forms of mountains and rivers, flowers and trees, supported the inheritance of memory.

Western monuments stood athwart the flow of time and the forms of nature, insisting on their own existence. One Dutchman who came to Nagasaki during the Edo period praised the beauty of the forested mountains surrounding the harbor and the mild waters of the bay, but then added, "There is only one thing missing, though—some kind of monument. Then the scene would be perfect." His comment clearly reflects the idea that monuments exist apart from nature, defying time and nature to transmit human memory forever. But in Japan, the same human memory resided less in durable materials and more in connections to time and the natural world.

Hiroshige's *Meisho Edo hyakkei* aptly illustrates the Japanese concept of *meisho*. The series of prints, which also functions as a kind of tourist guide to Edo, includes 118 *meisho* inside Edo, by then already a city of a million people. What is interesting is that virtually none of Hiroshige's images include anything that compares with the monuments that would certainly appear in the same project for a Western city. Above all, Edo Castle does not appear once, despite surely being the most important building in the city at the time. Hiroshige may have left it out because the residence of the shogun was not somewhere commoners could easily go. However, even in the print depicting Sensōji temple in Asakusa, a spot popular among Edoites and travelers alike, the all-important temple is a tiny, distant form, largely obscured by trees. The star of the image is the snow. In the same way, flowers or crimson leaves take center stage in prints like "Plum Estate, Kameido" (*Kameido umeyashiki*), "Suwa Bluff, Nippori" (*Suwa no dai, Nippori*), "Cherry Blossoms on the Tama River Embankment" (*Tamagawa-zutsumi no hana*), "Horikiri Iris Garden" (*Horikiri no hana-shōbu*), and "Autumn Leaves at Mama" (*Mama no momiji*). Snowy landscapes also appear in the first image of the series, "Fine Weather After Snow on Nihonbashi Bridge" (*Nihonbashi yukihare*), as well as in "Atagoshita and Yabu Lane" (*Atagoshita Yabukōji*), "Bikunibashi Bridge in Snow" (*Bikunibashi setchū*), and others. In many other prints, annual observances are the main theme, as discussed in an earlier chapter: New Year's kite-flying in "Kasumigaseki," carp streamers for the Children's Festival in the fifth month in "Suidobashi Bridge and Surugadai" (*Suidōbashi Surugadai*), the titular summer festival in "Flourishing City, Tanabata Festival" (*Shichū han'ei tanabata matsuri*), the late summer "Ryogoku Fireworks" (*Ryōgoku no hanabi*), and even "Fox Fires on New Year's Eve by the Shōzokuenoki Tree at Ōji" (*Ōji Shōzokuenoki ōmisoka no kitsunebi*), depicting a local legend about foxes gathering at the end of the year. Each title in the series refers to a *meisho*, but the main themes are less "views" or "places" than seasons and observances—or rather, only views and places with close ties to seasons and observances became *meisho*.

Even as Hiroshige depicts the *meisho* of the metropolis, he does not forget the nature that surrounds them. Western monuments towered amid the urban landscape, attracting the eye and becoming landmarks and symbols of the town. As far as we can tell from Hiroshige's *meisho*, however, Edo did not have this type of man-made structure. Indeed, after the Great Fire of Meireki (1657), Edo Castle did not have a keep. But Edo was not entirely without landmarks. In roughly a third of the images in *Meisho Edo hyakkei*, either Mount Fuji or Mount Tsukuba is clearly visible. Some of the prints even take Mount Fuji as the main subject, such as "Suruga-chō" (*Suruga-chō*) "New Mount Fuji in Meguro" (*Meguro Shinfuji*), and "Original Mount Fuji in Meguro" (*Meguro Motofuji*). Mount Fuji and Mount Tsukuba *were* landmarks to Edoites, just like the peaks to the east were to the residents of Kyoto. Alongside the seasons and annual observances, the natural landscape, too, took part in creating *meisho*.

An Important Message from Japan

To summarize, the inheritance of form and memory connected to place, season, and human activity has allowed Japanese culture to be transmitted in a manner quite unlike that of the West, where monuments play a central role. Not only has this linked people together through a common heritage, it has also driven the development of unique approaches to literature, art, and other creative endeavors based on the use of that heritage. This is why techniques like *honkadori* and *mitate*, which involve quotation and metaphor but are far more than this, have played such a crucial role in those fields. By becoming one member of a community of remembrance, artists enter into dialogue with countless predecessors, embracing that heritage while building realms of their own. Behind Bashō's seventeen-syllable haiku lie memories of the tanka poet Saigyō and works like the *Tales of Ise* and *Chronicle of Great Peace* (*Taiheiki*). At times, this goes so far as to almost become a collaboration with artists of bygone centuries.

Western artists, too, make use of their history. However, particularly from the Renaissance onward, artists largely utilized the past to separate themselves from others and create worlds complete in themselves—like, yes, monuments. In Japan, however, traditional forms were established that enabled dialogue not only with past artists but also contemporary ones. Colleagues gathered together to engage in artistic creation without relinquishing their individuality, through genres like *renga* (linked verse) and *renku* (linked haiku).

In the twentieth century, Ōoka Makoto pioneered a globally collaborative form called *renshi* (linked poetry) modeled on *renga* and *renku*. In *Renshi no tanoshimi* (The pleasures of *renshi*) he describes how unusual this "adventure in poetic co-creation" was for the Western poets who participated.[2] According to Ōoka, they found the experience by turns unsettling, disorienting, and even enraging. Octavio Paz, who participated at the invitation of Ōoka, called the several days he spent producing *renshi* "a trial—a little purgatory. . . . Between March 30 and April 3 [1969], what we discovered was our own humiliation."

However, that did not mean that Paz rejected collaborative poetry. Far from it: in forms like *renshi* and *renga* he saw the possibility of breaking through the Western cult of individuality. In the introduction to another book, he writes:

> The practice of the *renga* implies the negation of certain cardinal Western notions, such as the belief in the soul and the reality of the I. . . . Although it was governed by rules as strict as those of etiquette, its object was not to put a brake on spontaneity, but to open up a free space so that the genius of each one could manifest itself without doing harm either to others or to oneself.[3]

This comment from a Nobel laureate suggests that the traditions of Japanese culture that upheld the heritage of memory may have something to contribute to the rest of the world, just as the methods of cultural conservation employed at the Ise Grand Shrine are meaningful as a unique approach with no parallel in the West. (This is not, of course, to deny the great value of monument culture, or its impressive achievements.)

When I recently suggested that the shrine at Ise should be proposed for inclusion on the World Heritage List, I was informed that this was simply impossible under current circumstances. For something to be recognized as "World Heritage," it must first be formally declared part of its own nation's cultural heritage, with appropriate conservation measures in place. In Japan, designations like "National Treasure" and "Important Cultural Property" are made under the Law for the Protection of Cultural Properties. As it stands, this law restricts "modifying the current state" of a potential Cultural Property (except in emergencies and similar situations). Tearing down and rebuilding the entire shrine is a fairly radical case of "modifying the current form," and therefore the Ise Grand Shrine cannot be designated a Cultural Property under the law.

But as the foregoing clearly demonstrates, the twenty-year rhythm of the Ise Grand Shrine and its accompanying rituals and observances *are* the "current state." Would it not be possible to designate the regular rebuilding process itself, along with those rituals, within the framework of the law as it stands? It seems to me that recognizing this alternate way for culture to exist would send an important message from Japan to the world.

Notes

1. Takano Kiyoshi, *Ise Jingū no nazo* (Tokyo: Shōdensha, 1992).
2. Ōoka Makoto, *Renshi no tanoshimi* (Tokyo: Iwanami Shoten, 1991).
3. Octavio Paz, Jacques Roubaud, Edoardo Sanguineti, and Charles Tomlinson, *Renga: A Chain of Poems* (New York: George Braziller, 1971).

Afterword

This book is a collection of my writings from the last fifteen years about Japanese art and the relationship between Japanese and Western art history. Most of the contents were written with a non-Japanese reader in mind.

My original field of specialization was Western art history. However, during my first sojourn in France as a graduate student, my interest gradually expanded to Japanese art as well. This may have partly been a manifestation of the homesickness I felt living in an unfamiliar land, and I imagine that the questions I received about Japanese art from friends I made in France also had some effect on my thinking. Above all, however, I must credit a certain traveling exhibition of Japanese art that happened to open in Europe while I was there, in 1958. Not only was this exhibition my first contact with many of the Japanese masterpieces displayed, walking through the galleries with my European friends made me realize that our reactions to those artworks were subtly but unmistakably different. You might say that this was the first time I became aware of my Japanese identity.

This experience stayed with me for a long time, like a challenge I was bound to one day address. Adding early modern Japanese art history to my areas of study shortly after returning to Japan was my first step toward answering that challenge.

Since then, I have helped to organize a number of exhibitions involving Japanese art: *Autumn Grasses and Water* at the Japan House Gallery, New York, featuring works from the Suntory Museum of Art; *Avant-Garde Arts of Japan 1910–1970* at the Centre Pompidou, Paris; *Le japonisme* at the Grand Palais, also in Paris; and *Paris in Japan: The Japanese Encounter with European Painting*, which traveled across the United States. On these projects, I keenly felt the need to explain the history and characteristics of Japanese art to patrons from other countries. The contents of this book are the result of my attempts to do so.

These writings are no more than exploratory essays, of course, but comparing Japanese art to the art of other countries, particularly European countries, can reveal characteristics that we had not noticed before, and even spur us to contemplation of deeper matters involving the respective essences of Japanese and European culture. In this sense, writing these essays was a deeply rewarding task for me. I am delighted beyond measure that Iwanami Shoten has now collected them into a single volume.

I am sincerely grateful to the many people who assisted in the creation of this book. I offer particular thanks to all the exhibition curators and editors who invited me to write on these topics, as well as my colleague Tsuji Nobuo and other specialists in Japanese art history who offered me guidance on countless points. For the editing of this book, I am indebted to Satō Taeko of Iwanami Shoten.

Takashina Shūji

October 1991

Afterword to the Expanded Edition

"A thing of beauty is a joy forever": so wrote John Keats in the now-famous opening line of *Endymion*. Indeed, contact with beauty brings joy that never changes; this, I imagine, is common to every human heart. However, the same cannot be said for our understanding of what actually constitutes a "thing of beauty." The sheer variety of the forms of beauty birthed by the human race in different ages and places—sometimes differing to the point of mutual incomprehension—speaks eloquently to this. The human sense of beauty is nurtured by cultural and historical conditions as well as the accumulation of individual experience.

Some differences, of course, are greater than others. Consider English art historian Nikolaus Pevsner's worthy tome *The Englishness of English Art*, companion volumes of which could easily be written on the "Frenchness of French art," or the "Italianness of Italian art." And yet, compared to the arts of Asia or Africa, those of England, France, and Italy do share a certain character as "European art." The situation is similar regarding the "Japaneseness of Japanese art": amid the commonalities with continental China, the Korean Peninsula, and other parts of Asia—particularly the East Asian cultural sphere to which Japan belongs—the works of beauty produced by the Japanese over the past millennium and a half nevertheless have certain characteristics that form a common thread, and which can surely be identified with the unique aesthetic sensibilities of the Japanese people.

This book was originally published in 1991 as a collection of essays written from this perspective for a variety of venues and occasions. This expanded edition adds two new essays. One discusses how Japanese artists have expressed the four seasons, a topic deeply related to the Japanese view of nature, and the other is about "duets" of word and image. Both are attempts to elucidate the essence of Japanese culture as expressed not only in visual art but also in literature.

I would like to offer my deepest gratitude to Iwanami Shoten for agreeing to publish both the original edition and this expanded one, and particularly to Nakanishi Sawako, chief editor of the Gendai Bunko series in which this edition is included.

Takashina Shūji
November 2009

Original Publication Details

I: Methods of Japanese Art

The Character of Japanese Aesthetics. As "The Japanese Sense of Beauty" in *Autumn Grasses and Water: Motifs in Japanese Art*. New York: Japan Society, 1983. Catalog published in conjunction with an exhibition of the same title, organized by the Suntory Museum of Art and the Japan Society.

Object and Form. As "Jānaru bunmei ronpyō: Mono no shisō to kata no shisō" in *Tsūsan jānaru*, December 1978.

Forms of Seeing, East and West. As "Nihon no bijutsu" in *Nihonjin no kachikan*. Kōza: Hikaku bunka, vol. 7. Tokyo: Kenkyūsha, 1976.

The "Trailing Bough" Motif. As "Sora kara furu eda: Shidare motīfu ron" in *Bijutsushi ronsō* 5, 1989.

The Art of the Journey. As "E no tabi/tabi no e" in *Kikan Nihon no bigaku* 1, 1984.

The Principle of Ornamentation. As "Nihonjin no biteki nōryoku: Sōshokusei no genri" in *Kokusai kōryū* 53, 1990.

II: East-West Encounters

East and West in Meiji Painting. As "Eastern and Western Dynamics in the Development of Western-Style Oil Painting during the Meiji Era" in *Paris in Japan: The Japanese Encounter with European Painting*, edited by Takashina Shūji, J. Thomas Rimer, and Gerald D. Bolas. St. Louis: Washington University, 1987. Catalog published in conjunction with an exhibition of the same title.

The Avant-Garde in Japanese Art. As "Japon des avant-gardes" in *Japon des avant-gardes: 1910–1970*. Paris: Centre Pompidou, 1987. Catalog published in conjunction with an exhibition of the same title.

Japanese Academism. As "Kanōha no 'akademizumu'" in *Edo-Tōkyō 400-nen kinen ten katarogu*. Tokyo: Tokyo Metropolitan Teien Art Museum, 1989. Introduction to catalog published in conjunction with an exhibition of the same title.

Some Problems of *Japonisme*. As "Japonisumu no shomondai" in *Japonisumu-ten katarogu*. Tokyo: National Museum of Western Art, 1988. Catalog published in conjunction with an exhibition of the same title, organized by the National Museum of Western Art, Japan Foundation, Japan Broadcasting Corporation, and Yomiuri Shinbun.

III: Passing Beauty, Returning Memory

The Aesthetics of Transition: The Four Seasons and the Japanese Sense of Beauty. As "Utsuroi no bigaku: Shiki to Nihonjin no biishiki" in *Nihon no bi III: Nihon no shiki, haru/natsu*. Tokyo: Bijutsu Nenkansha, 2008.

"The Color of the Flowers": Symphonies of Image and Word. Written for this volume.

The Heritage of Memory: Intangible Culture as Japanese Tradition. As "Kioku no isan: Mukei no bunka to iu Nihon no dentō" in *Chūo Kōron*, October 1996.

About the Author

Takashina Shūji is an art historian, art critic, professor emeritus at the University of Tokyo, director of the Ohara Museum of Art, and president of the Japan Art Academy.

Born in 1932, he graduated from the University of Tokyo's College of Arts and Sciences and went on to study modern Western art history at the Sorbonne and the École du Louvre. His previously held positions include professor at the University of Tokyo and director general of the National Museum of Western Art. He received the Medal of Honor with Purple Ribbon in 2000, was named Chevalier of the French Legion of Honor in 2001, and was awarded the Japan Art Academy Prize and Imperial Prize from the Japan Art Academy in 2002. He was recognized by the Japanese government as a Person of Cultural Merit in 2005, and inducted into the Order of Culture in 2012. In 2015, he was appointed to the Japan Art Academy, and in 2020 he was made academy president.

Other books by Takashina include, in English, *The Japanese Sense of Beauty* (JPIC) and, in Japanese, *Seikimatsu geijutsu* (Fin-de-Siècle Art, Chikuma Gakugei Bunko), *Runessansu no hikari to yami* (Light and Dark in the Renaissance, Chūkō Bunko), *Nihon kindai bijutsushi-ron* (A History of Modern Art in Japan, Chikuma Gakugei Bunko), *Kindai kaigaishi: Goya kara Mondorian made* (A History of Modern Painting: From Goya to Mondrian, Chūkō Shinsho, in two volumes), *Pikaso: Hyōsetsu no ronri* (Picasso: The Logic of Plagiarism, Chikuma Gakugei Bunko), *20 seiki bijutsu* (20th-Century Art, Chikuma Gakugei Bunko), *Seiyō no me, Nihon no me* (The Western Eye, the Japanese Eye, Seidosha), and *Miro no Viinasu wa naze kessaku ka?* (Why Is the Venus de Milo a Masterpiece?, Shōgakukan).

About The Translator

Matt Treyvaud is an Australian-born translator who lives south of Tokyo. His other translations for Japan Library include Takashina Shūji's *The Japanese Sense of Beauty* and Shimura Fukumi's *The Music of Color*.

（英文版）増補 日本美術を見る眼 東と西の出会い
Japanese Art in Perspective: East-West Encounters

2021 年 3 月 27 日　第 1 刷発行

著　者　高階秀爾
訳　者　マット・トライヴォー
発行所　一般財団法人出版文化産業振興財団
　　　　〒 101-0051 東京都千代田区神田神保町 2-2-30
　　　　電話　03-5211-7283
　　　　ホームページ　https://www.jpic.or.jp/

印刷・製本所　大日本印刷株式会社